HISTORY:
POLITICS
— OR —
CULTURE?

HISTORY: POLITICS
=== OR ===
CULTURE?

REFLECTIONS ON
Ranke and Burckhardt

FELIX GILBERT

PRINCETON UNIVERSITY PRESS

Published by Princeton University Press, 41 William Street,
Princeton, New Jersey 08540
In the United Kingdom: Princeton University Press, Oxford

All Rights Reserved

Library of Congress Cataloging-in-Publication Data

Gilbert, Felix, 1905-
History : politics or culture? : reflections on Ranke and Burckhardt
/ Felix Gilbert.
p. cm.
Includes index.
ISBN 0-691-03163-0 (alk. paper)
1. History—Philosophy. 2. Ranke, Leopold von, 1795-1886—
Contributions in the philosophy of history. 3. Burckhardt, Jacob,
1818–1897—Contributions in the philosophy of history. I. Title.
D16.8.G532 1990
901—dc20   90-37417   CIP

This book has been composed in Trump Medieval

Princeton University Press books are printed on acid-free paper,
and meet the guidelines for permanence and durability of the
Committee on Production Guidelines for Book Longevity
of the Council on Library Resources

Printed in the United States of America by
Princeton University Press, Princeton, New Jersey

1   3   5   7   9   10   8   6   4   2

FOR
Leonard Krieger

▼

CONTENTS

PREFACE

THE TWO historians whose writings and ideas are discussed in this volume have been important for my work since the 1920s. In my dissertation, which was concerned with Johann Gustav Droysen, Ranke's main competitor among German historians, Ranke's influence on the development of modern historiography had to be discussed; when I then turned in my work to the history of the Italian Renaissance, unavoidably the questions that Burckhardt's analysis of this period had raised became centers of my attention.

When, in 1981, as guest professor at Stanford Univesity I offered a seminar on nineteenth-century historiography, I became attracted by the idea of a more detailed study of Ranke's and Burckhardt's thought. In reading the recent interesting literature on Ranke and Burckhardt I grew intrigued by two questions that seemed to me unsatisfactorily treated. The one was the relation of Ranke's view of historical scholarship to the notions on the aims and purposes of history that had been developed in the eighteenth century; to put it briefly: what was really new in Ranke? Concerning Burckhardt there exists a rich literature of outstanding quality, but the problem that seems to have been somewhat slighted, or at least not to have been discussed appropriately, contains the question of the relation in which his idea of history stood to the political and scholarly trends of his time, and to what extent his concept of cultural history was formed in reaction to them. These are the questions that stand behind this collection of essays.

Two of the essays in this book have been published before—the third in the *American Scholar* of summer 1987, and the sixth, which appears here by permission of the publisher, in *Leopold von Ranke and the Shaping of the Historical Discipline*, edited by Georg G. Iggers and James M. Powell, 82–88 (Syracuse: Syracuse University Press, 1990); they are republished with only slight changes. Ideas informing some of the other essays have been presented at meetings of the American Philosophical Society, of the Renaissance Society of America, of the Davis Seminar of Princeton University, and at Brown University. They appear in this book in a widely extended and thoroughly revised version.

I have mentioned that this collection of essays owes its origin to an invitation from Stanford University, and I wish to thank the members of the Stanford History Department for an unusually stimulating term. I also wish to thank the State Archives in Basel, where I was permitted to study the papers of Jacob Burckhardt, and the Director of the Herzog August Bibliothek in Wolfenbüttel, where I made use of its unrivaled treasures of eighteenth-century literature. Finally, Mary Gilbert, Christoph and Flora Kimmich, Arno Mayer, Peter Paret, and Fritz Stern were kind enough to look at the manuscript and to give me helpful criticisms.

HISTORY:
POLITICS
— OR —
CULTURE?

CHAPTER I

THE IMPACT OF THE FRENCH REVOLU-
TION AND OF THE NAPOLEONIC
AGE ON HISTORICAL
THOUGHT

T HE REVOLUTION has created a connected unity
that distinguishes our time from earlier times.
Jacob Burckhardt opened his lecture course on
the "History of the Revolutionary Age"[1] with this
statement, which expressed a view widely held in the
nineteenth century. To a large extent it is still held
and has had a great impact on the study of the past: it
widened the historical outlook and gave new importance to an old problem, the problem of historical continuity. The question that had arisen was this: If the
French Revolution created an era different from all earlier periods, did knowledge of the past have any value,
and did any bonds remain between former times and
the postrevolutionary age? To historians in particular,
the relation of this modern period to the preceding
centuries was a question of crucial interest, and for
them the establishment of the characteristic features
of the recent past was of decisive importance in the
study of history. Significantly, three of the leading

[1] See *Jacob Burckhardt's Vorlesung über die Geschichte des Re-
volutionszeitalters*, reconstructed by Ernst Ziegler (Basel, 1974),
13: "Die Revolution hat einen ganzen Zusammenhang geschaffen,
durch welchen sie sich von der früheren Zeit unterscheidet."

German nineteenth-century historians—Ranke, Droysen, and Burckhardt—devoted particular efforts to courses on the recent past.

In the second year of his Berlin professorship, in 1826, Ranke taught a course on "Most Recent History from 1789 to 1815,"[2] and he continued to lecture on this topic in the following decades. In 1840 the young Johann Gustav Droysen, who had made a name for himself through a daring biography of Alexander the Great, became professor of history at Kiel University; in his second year he presented a lecture course on "The Wars of Liberation."[3] In 1858, Jacob Burckhardt became professor of history in his hometown, Basel, and began teaching courses on the Middle Ages and the Renaissance, historical periods with which his research had been primarily concerned. A year later, however, he was already offering a course on "The History of the Revolutionary Age."

The attention that was given to the period of the Revolution and of Napoleon indicates the overwhelming nature of the events of these years and their effect on the evolution of historical thinking. The titles of Ranke's, Droysen's, and Burckhardt's courses also show that each judged the effects differently. Ranke and Burckhardt viewed these decades as a period of crisis that revealed the dangers to which European society and culture were exposed. Droysen, more optimistic, regarded the period as disclosing the road to the future.

[2] "Neueste Geschichte von 1789 bis 1815."
[3] See Johann Gustav Droysen, *Vorlesungen über das Zeitalter der Freiheitskriege*, 2d ed. (Gotha, 1886), vii.

Droysen's lectures on "The Wars of Liberation" do not focus on the wars of the years 1812-1815 that brought about the downfall of Napoleon. The war of liberation with which his course began was the struggle of the English colonies in North America for independence. This revolt indicated that the time had come to subject the steadily increasing power of the state to the will of the people. For Droysen, constitutionalism and national independence dominated the age. The French Revolution and Napoleon's despotism warned of the difficulties and dangers involved in attainment of these aims. Yet the Revolution was also a turning point; it signified that a development toward national states in whose government the people participated could no longer be halted. For Droysen there was no inevitability in the future course of history, but he did have confidence in progress, in man's ability to improve social life. One might find in Droysen's optimistic beliefs a reflection of Hegel's philosophy of history, which exerted such a powerful influence in the earlier part of the nineteenth century. In any case, by emphasizing the gradual rise of national consciousness and constitutionalism, Droysen had no difficulty in integrating the events of the revolutionary period into the broader stream of historical development.

This task was much more difficult for Ranke and Burckhardt. Both were conservatives and their attitudes toward liberal and democratic movements were thoroughly negative. Certainly Ranke saw in the Revolution an event of decisive importance for the development of history, but not because it had brought novel ideas or new forces into political life. Rather the struggle of the revolutionary forces against the ruling classes and the established social structure had tested the strength of the existing institutions, had rejuvenated them and given them "greater fullness, higher importance and wider extent."[4] Burckhardt's view about the impact and the consequences of the French Revolution was most pessimistic: the Revolution had created a permanent crisis in the modern world. The idea of equality in law and economics and the extension of state power undermined all the previously existing forms of life, thus awakening a spirit of greed and criticism.[5]

As distinctive, even contradictory, as these evaluations of the significance of the French Revolution were, they all have a common element and confirm the statement by Burckhardt quoted at the chapter's opening: they all tended to see a connection among political, economic, and intellectual movements, and to place the developments that took place within an individual state in a broader European context. No doubt historians had always been curious about a great variety of human activities, but a consequence of the French Revolution was awareness of their interaction.

The period of the French Revolution not only widened the field of the historian; it also added a new aspect to existing notions about the forces shaping the course of historical events. In this respect it is critical

[4] From Ranke's essay "The Great Powers"; see the translation of this essay in Theodore H. Von Laue, *Leopold von Ranke: The Formative Years* (Princeton, 1950), 217. If in the following the origin of a translation from Ranke or Burckhardt is not indicated, the translation is my own; in such case the original German text is usually given in the footnote.

[5] See the "Einleitung" to his *Vorlesung*; he expresses similar opinions in his letters.

to give due weight to the fact that the period which opened the modern age was not only the era of the French Revolution but also the Age of Napoleon. It is difficult for us to grasp the overwhelming impression Napoleon made in the time of his triumphal successes. The tawdry glitter of the rule of Napoleon's nephew has tarnished the splendor of the first Napoleon's achievements, and the artificially constructed popularity of the fascist dictators has made it yet more difficult for us to appreciate the significance, at the beginning of the nineteenth century, of an individual's rise to the heights of power. In his years of triumphant progress Napoleon was for Goethe "a splendid and majestic figure." When Hegel saw Napoleon in Jena he believed he had seen "the universal spirit" riding in the town. The lectures on the French Revolution of Ranke, Droysen, and Burckhardt are a powerful reminder of the impression Napoleon made. Although Napoleon's failure to become the ruler of Europe was highly significant for Ranke's views of European history, still Napoleon was for him "the most grandiose phenomenon that we have seen passing before us."[6] For Droysen "a greater general, a more farseeing ruler never existed; one can never admire enough the boldness and magnificence of his views, the keenness of his mind. . . . He is a giant of human talent."[7] Burckhardt's view of Napoleon strangely combined admiration for the uniqueness of his gifts and rejection of his aims. "The picture he has left us is that of the most enormous individual strength in everything that

[6] Ranke, *Aus Werk und Nachlass*, ed. W. P. Fuchs and T. Schieder (Munich, 1975), 4:309.

[7] Droysen, *Vorlesungen*, 2:243.

touches upon the exercise of power. This is a picture like no one else's in world history. Such a man existed and swallowed up all glory. . . . But perhaps there exists still another glory than that of Napoleon."[8]

The decisive influence that Napoleon's rise and fall has exerted on the historical imagination worked in two rather different directions. Napoleon's failure revealed the weight and strength of forces that had created and preserved bonds in social life beyond the institutional structure of society. Napoleon's regime had shown that the feelings of common nationality and the ties of intellectual and religious conviction could not be overcome by outside pressure. This realization strengthened interest in history's capacity to build a bridge between the past and present, directing attention to factors that have shaped similarity and differences among the various European nations. The deepest impression that Napoleon had left was a new awareness of the power and possibilities inherent in human individuality. Napoleon had been able to break through the established and recognized social hierarchy and had thereby shaken belief in the authority of society's rulers and in their exertion of power by divine right. Napoleon's career seemed to show that an individual's intentions, insights, and will can direct events; it threw doubts, thereby, on the existence of a preordained course of history. History and philosophy began to draw apart. Whatever the importance of ideas for the development of history, its future course could no longer be deduced from speculations about the rational nature of man and the all-pervasive rule of reason. The notion of a predetermined course of world

[8] Burckhardt, *Vorlesung*, 420–421.

history seemed increasingly to have become a meaningless construction.

But through increased emphasis on historical reality the historian's field of interest was widened. The importance that had to be given to an individual and to his responsibility for historical action made an investigation of the reasons for the action undertaken an essential part of historical investigation. The historian had to make himself cognizant of the various possibilities that had existed. Since the late seventeenth and the eighteenth century the interest of historical writers in the use of primary sources had grown. But the new importance given to the individual's role in the making of a decision intensified the study of the conditions and attitudes involved in its formation. A new view about the factors determining the course of history developed, as well as a new attitude toward historical sources.

The impact of the events that had shaken the European world was not limited, however, to increased awareness of the interconnection existing among the forces working in history or to a widened knowledge of the factors which influenced the course of events. The historian himself had acquired a new role. His task was no longer restricted to recording the events of the past; he was seen as being in possession of a special knowledge regarding the way man acted in social life. His voice was expected to be heard in public life. It is significant that in the nineteenth century in almost all European countries many of the active politicians were historians and that from this group came a number of leading statesmen.[9]

[9] Guizot, Macaulay, Mommsen, Rotteck, and Thiers, among others.

The understanding of history that arose under the impact of the quarter century from the fall of the Bastille to the overthrow of Napoleon evolved gradually and in different ways, depending on the particular situation in the various European countries. The influence of the age of the Revolution and of Napoleon is undeniable and was particularly strong in Germany. The years of Napoleon's domination had deeply shaken and changed the social structure and the political institutions there. But the period of restoration that followed Napoleon's defeat checked and restricted these reforms. The situation that had developed was basically unstable and could not last. It was almost inevitable that some would look to history for an answer to the question: What are the permanent forces on which society could be securely built?

CHAPTER II

·▼▼▼▏▏▏▏▏▏▏▏▼▼·

RANKE'S VIEW OF THE TASK OF HIS-
TORICAL SCHOLARSHIP

L EOPOLD VON RANKE'S influence on the development
of historical scholarship has been the subject of
many books and articles.[1] The result of these in-
vestigations—which in the course of the nineteenth
century became a widely accepted dogma—was that
by using a new method, the philological-critical
method, Ranke raised history to a science. A consequence was that the historian's primary concern ought
to be political history based on the analysis of archival
material. This view of Ranke's importance and influence has its dangers, because this nineteenth-century
image simplifies and rigidifies Ranke's contribution to
the study of history. We may come to a better understanding of Ranke's importance for the history of his-

[1] Leopold von Ranke, *The Theory and Practice of History*, ed.
Georg G. Iggers and Konrad von Moltke (New York, 1973), contains
on pp. lxxiii-lxxx a "Bibliographical Note" that lists the major writings on Ranke; but for the most recent literature, see the two books
published on the occasion of the centenary of Ranke's death: *Leopold von Ranke und die moderne Geschichtswissenschaft*, ed.
W. J. Mommsen (Stuttgart, 1988), and *Leopold von Ranke and the
Shaping of the Historical Discipline*, ed. Georg G. Iggers and James
M. Powell (Syracuse, 1990). For an example of the influence of the
rigidified conception of Ranke's influence, see my paper, "Leopold
von Ranke and the American Philosophical Society," *Proceedings
of the American Philosophical Society* 130, no. 3 (September 1986):
362–366.

toriography when we examine why, as soon as Ranke's first work appeared, it stood out from the work done by his contemporaries and directed wide attention to this young teacher at a provincial Gymnasium.

Ranke's first work, the two volumes of the *Histories of the Latin and Teutonic Nations*, appeared in 1824.[2] With the publication of this work, Ranke's meteoric rise in the academic world began. In March of the following year he was appointed professor at the University of Berlin; two years later the Prussian government gave him financial support so that he could spend the next three years in Vienna and Italy pursuing archival research. After his return to Berlin, Ranke was well received in Berlin's literary and academic circles and was particularly close to the small but important group of anti-Hegelians. From 1832 on, for four years, Ranke edited the *Historisch-Politische Zeitschrift*, a literary enterprise that the government had initiated to represent its political views to the public. During these years the first of his masterpieces, *The History of the Popes*, began to appear. Thus, ten years after the publication of his first historical work, Ranke was recognized as a leading historian in the German intellectual world.[3]

[2] In the following, quotations are based on the first edition of *Geschichten der romanischen und germanischen Völker von 1494 bis 1535* (Leipzig and Berlin, 1824). I shall refer to the first volume as *Geschichten der*, and I shall cite the second volume, *Zur Kritik Neuerer Geschichtschreiber*, as *Zur Kritik*.

[3] For a recent comprehensive analysis of Ranke's first historical work, which places this work within a broad picture of Ranke's intellectual development, see "Rankes Erstlingswerk oder der Beginn der kritischen Geschichtsschreibung über die Neuzeit," in Ernst Schulin, *Traditionskritik und Rekonstruktionsversuch* (Göttingen, 1979), 44–64. For Ranke's early development, see Hermann

I.

In Ranke's *Histories of the Latin and Teutonic Nations* the reader becomes aware of an aim that Ranke carried out increasingly successful in his later writings: that of making the writing of history a literary art.[4] Throughout his life Ranke never lost sight of the view he expressed at the beginning of his career: "History differs from all other scholarly activities by being also an art."[5] The style of the *Histories of the Latin and Teutonic Nations* immediately aroused attention, but judgment was by no means unanimous: some praised the style and others criticized its artificiality. Style was certainly a striking feature of the work, but the contradictory reaction is understandable. There are bleak passages, overcrowded with details, but there are also brilliant portraits of the leading actors. For example, a description of Raphael's portrait of Julius II serves as an insight into the policies of this pope.[6] Ranke uses literary devices to differentiate the importance of the events he describes. The irrelevance of certain struggles among the Swiss cantons is indicated by his inserted observation, "In the midst between them flowed the Rhine and adorned the banks

---

Oncken, *Aus Rankes Frühzeit* (Gotha, 1922), and Theodore H. von Laue, *Leopold Ranke: The Formative Years* (Princeton, 1950).

[4] This issue is discussed in Hermann von der Dunk, "Die historische Darstellung bei Ranke: Literatur und Wissenschaft," in *Leopold von Ranke und die moderne Geschichtswissenschaft*, ed. Wolfgang Mommsen (Stuttgart, 1988), 131–165. The article by von der Dunk also refers to the recent relevant literature.

[5] Leopold von Ranke, *Aus Werk und Nachlass*, ed. W. P. Fuchs and T. Schieder, vol. 4, *Vorlesungseinleitungen* (Munich, 1975), 72.

[6] *Geschichten der*, 274.

on both sides with the splendor of spring."[7] Ranke himself realized that in his first work he had gone rather far in his attempt to arouse attention by his style, and in later works he used literary devices chiefly when they contributed to an understanding of the causal connection between events.

When Ranke's first book appeared, historical writings were not expected to be works of literary art. Most German historians were content with a more or less factual presentation. There was one famous exception, Johannes von Müller. Müller was a prominent figure in the literary as well as in the scholarly world whose work was universally admired. Ranke referred frequently to Müller's writings, and it has been suggested that he named his own first book "Histories" and not "History" in imitation of Müller's *Histories of the Swiss Confederation*. In his old age Ranke acknowledged that, from his youth on, Müller had stood before him as "a model of diligence, of penetrating perception as well as of succinct expression."[8] Certainly the first work of the young Ranke raised the hope that a successor of Johannes von Müller was coming forth. It is a remarkable coincidence that in the winter of 1824/25 Ranke found in Johannes von Müller's writings a note which directed his attention to the Venetian diplomatic reports, the "Relazioni." Ranke's interpretation of these documents would form the foundation of modern historical scholarship based on new principles and methods.[9]

[7] Ibid., 143.

[8] Leopold von Ranke, *Neue Briefe*, ed. Bernhard Hoeft (Hamburg, 1949), 480: February 26, 1867.

[9] Leopold von Ranke, *Das Briefwerk*, ed. W. P. Fuchs (Hamburg, 1949), 84 n. 4.

II.

Ranke's *Histories of the Latin and Teutonic Nations* consists of two volumes; the second is a supplement containing a critical examination and evaluation of the sources used in establishing the narrative account contained in the first. From the outset much scholarly interest focused on this supplementary volume, and its analysis of sixteenth-century historians has always been recognized as the first indication of Ranke's critical method. A consideration of the message contained in this volume is crucial, therefore, to our exploration of what is new in Ranke.

Most of the analyses of the historians and their works are rather brief. At the beginning and at the end of the volume, however, we find two articles whose length indicates their particular importance. It is ironic that we now regard these two studies written by the recognized innovator of critical historical scholarship as misinterpretations. The long introductory essay is a condemnation of the *History of Italy* by Guicciardini, whom Ranke presents as a self-serving falsifier and even inventor of facts. The last article of the book has the merit of placing Machiavelli's political thought in the context of the political and intellectual situation of his time, but it underplays the role of personal ambition and humanistic rhetoric in shaping *The Prince* and the *Discorsi*. An explanation of the passionate zeal with which Ranke attacked Guicciardini and defended Machiavelli lies in the fact that Ranke's views were contradictory to the prevailing opinion. Guicciardini was typically seen as "contemporary, participant, and impartial narrator and judge of

events,"[10] and Machiavelli had not yet emerged from
the accusations of moral depravity that the anti-Ma-
chiavellians had raised. Yet even if in his analyses of
Guicciardini and Machiavelli Ranke went too far in
his critical enthusiasm, these two evaluations are revealing testimonies of the approach he took in subjecting a historical source to critical examination.

In the course of the eighteenth century certain basic
standards had been established regarding the attitude a
historian should take toward his subject and the evaluation of material to be used.[11] The historian should
be impartial and his search ought to be guided by
truthfulness. In order to be true the picture had to be
precise and complete. The reliability of the reports the
historian uses varies, and so the value of a source depends largely on the proximity of its author to the
event he described. Memoirs of statesmen and reports
of participants are especially valuable. It was recognized that the documentary material that originates in
the course of an action is particularly authentic, but at
the time of Ranke's beginnings the archives in which
the documentary material was kept were often inac-
cessible.

Ranke was aware of the recognized standards of historical scholarship as they had been developed in the
eighteenth century, but he extended the method of
historical criticism. While Ranke's contemporaries
based their histories on the accounts of earlier histori-

[10] Guicciardini is characterized this way in Arnold Heeren,
Handbuch der Geschichte des Europäischen Staatensystems (Göttingen, 1819), 1:23.

[11] On the "Gesetze der kritischen Forschung," see, for instance,
Ludwig Wachler, *Geschichte der historischen Forschung und Kunst*
(Göttingen, 1812), 1:344f.

ans who were recognized authorities, and their critical method consisted largely in correcting errors or in adding information that the study of other sources had revealed, Ranke believed the sources warranted a much more rigorous examination. As his analysis of Guicciardini's and Machiavelli's writings shows, he saw a close connection between the personality of a writer and the account he presented. Each account reflects the intellectual formation, the situation, and the interests of its writer and was shaped by the ideas and aims of the world in which he lived and acted. As Ranke formulated it a few years later, "Every writing, not only its value and importance, but in a certain sense its life, depends on the relationship between subject and object, between author and his topic. The first task of every critical examination is to make this relation visible."[12] What a writer presented was *his* picture of the events. It could help to establish what actually had happened, but it had to be placed in relation to all the other sources that deal with the same period and the same events. What sources report about the past cannot be accepted as fact; the establishment of the facts is the work of the historian, who must reconstruct them on the basis of all the available material.

Ranke's demand for a more extended and more intense critical examination of the historical sources corresponds to developments that were taking place in

[12] *Jahrbücher des Deutschen Reiches unter dem Sächsischen Hause*, ed. Leopold Ranke (Berlin, 1837), 1:v: "Eine jede Schrift, nicht allein ihr Werth und ihre Bedeutung, sondern in gewissem Sinne ihr Dasein selbst beruht auf dem Verhältniss zwischen Subject und Object, zwischen dem Verfasser und seinem Gegenstand. Wie alle Kritik zuletzt die Aufgabe haben wird dies Verhältniss zur Anschauung zu bringen."

the scholarship of the time. Ranke had studied classical philology under one of the great masters in this field: Barthold Georg Niebuhr. In lectures given almost thirty years after the appearance of the *Histories of the Latin and Teutonic Nations*, Ranke called Niebuhr's work "a model of the method of historical research."[13] In subjecting the writings of earlier historians to his sharpened and thorough method of historical criticism, Ranke indeed followed Niebuhr, who had rejected the histories of the Roman kings and had reconstructed the beginnings of Roman history through consideration of the concrete conditions of economic life.

By making the establishment of the facts of the past the main aim of historical criticism, Ranke set up a clear priority among the sources of history. The first place belonged to archival research. Although the importance of archival sources had always been recognized, their unique value, distinguishing them from other sources, was now acknowledged. From this point on we can observe historians increasing pressure to gain access to archival material until the archives became the basic element in historical research.

Modern history is considered to have been the area of Ranke's interest. His chief works do not go back further than to the age of the Renaissance and of the Reformation. Yet the first great historical enterprise he inspired, which became the common endeavor of the first generation of his disciples, was concerned with medieval history: *The Yearbooks of the German Em-*

[13] A detailed evaluation of Niebuhr by Ranke will be found in *Aus Werk und Nachlass*, 4:227–230; see also *Das Briefwerk*, 229, 296.

pire. In the first volume's preface Ranke explained its purpose: the source material of the Middle Ages was daily increasing; the "next necessity, therefore, was to establish the facts in chronological order."[14] The *Yearbooks* realized the basic idea of the tasks of historical criticism.

III.

The idea that establishing the facts of the past is the historian's foremost duty is quite explicitly and categorically stated at various places in the *Histories of the Latin and Teutonic Nations*. The preface of the book contains the most famous of these statements: "To history has been assigned the task of judging the past, of instructing the world of today for the benefit of future years. The present attempt does not claim such an exalted function; it merely wants to state what actually happened."[15] Ranke underlines this statement's importance by returning to it later in the same preface. "Strict description of the fact, although it might limit us and prove to be unpleasant, is without doubt the supreme law."[16] And finally at a crucial place in his analysis of Guicciardini's *History of Italy*—as he begins to discuss events that in Ranke's opinion Guicciardini distorted or invented—Ranke asserts, "We on our side have a different concept of history: Naked

[14] *Jahrbücher*, 1:xi.

[15] *Geschichten der*, v. "Man hat der Historie das Amt, die Vergangenheit zu richten, die Mitwelt zum Nutzen zukünftiger Jahre zu belehren, beygemessen: so hoher Aemter unterwindet sich gegenwärtiger Versuch nicht: er will bloss sagen, wie es eigentlich gewesen."

[16] Ibid., vii. "Strenge Darstellung der Thatsache, wie bedingt und unschön sie auch sey, ist ohne Zweifel das oberste Gesetz."

truth, without embellishment, through an investigation of the individual fact, the rest left to God, but no poeticizing, no fantasizing."[17]

The last statement is particularly significant. Insisting on the need to explore fully and thoroughly the possibilities of historical criticism, Ranke wanted to do more than eliminate errors from the account of the past. The historian, he believed, had to present a new account of the past consisting of the facts that he had established. This demand for a critical historical method was intended to achieve more than a technical improvement in the writing of history; it reflected the impact of new ideas about the nature and value of historical scholarship.

History was an autonomous discipline; this was the core of the new concept of history on which Ranke's work was founded. He claimed a place for history in the university structure that it had never previously held. Certainly, histories had always been written, but their purposes had varied widely: from pure amusement to ethical and political instruction.[18] Because of

[17] *Zur Kritik*, 28. "Wir unsers Orts haben einen andern Begriff von Geschichte. Nackte Wahrheit ohne allen Schmuck; gründliche Erforschung des Einzelnen; das Uebrige Gott befohlen; nur kein Erdichten, auch nicht im Kleinsten, nur kein Hirngespinst."

[18] On recent research regarding the nature of eighteenth-century concern with history, see *Aufklärung und Geschichte*, ed. Hans Erich Bödeker, Georg G. Iggers, Jonathan B. Knudsen, and Peter H. Reill (Göttingen, 1986), particularly the article by Rudolf Vierhaus, "Historisches Interesse im 18. Jahrhundert," 264–275. See also *Von der Aufklärung zum Historismus*, ed. Hans Walter Blanke and Jörn Rüsen (Paderborn, 1984), especially the contribution by Blanke, "Aufklärungshistorie, Historismus und historische Kritik," 167–186. I cannot deny that, in my opinion, the recent discovery of historical interest in eighteenth-century Germany has led to an overestimation of the importance of this "progress."

the variety of purposes that history served it had been assigned no autonomous role in the university curriculum. Chairs devoted exclusively to the teaching of history did not exist at German universities.

University students gained a knowledge of the past in the teachings of the theological and law faculties; and in the philosophical faculty history was often used to supply examples in the teaching of rhetoric and ethics. As the eighteenth century progressed historical lectures came to be more frequently offered in the philosophical faculties. For instance, at the University of Göttingen, where particular attention was given to the teaching of history, courses were offered on "older" and "more recent" universal history, on a history of the European states in the seventeenth and eighteenth centuries, and on special histories of one or the other of the German states. In addition auxiliary sciences, like geography, chronology, diplomatics, heraldry, and numismatics, were taught.[19] Outside the universities there was a growing public interest in history, as witnessed by articles in periodicals and in the publications of the academies.

Despite this interest in expanding historical knowledge, however, history remained chiefly a subsidiary pursuit that served the purposes of other spheres of life. Ranke's famous statement in the preface of the *Histories of the Latin and Teutonic Nations* must be placed in this context as a challenge to the prevailing views. Ranke drew a line between what his predecessors and contemporaries attempted to achieve with

[19] See *Versuch einer Akademischen Gelehrtengeschichte von der Georg Augustus Universität zu Göttingen* (Göttingen, 1765); for a listing of the historical lectures given in Göttingen, see 302–305. For a few years a historical academy even existed in Göttingen.

their historical work and what his own aim was. For him history was an autonomous discipline equal to all the others.

Ranke's thesis of history's autonomy formed part of the new ideas about the role of the university and university teaching that had found expression in Humboldt's foundation of the University of Berlin in 1810. Particularly the philosophical faculty had gained in stature because it was here that scholars were to devote themselves to their true purpose: the search for truth about man and nature. Man could never attain the full truth, but in his own particular field, with the methods appropriate to discoveries in this field, he could contribute to the continuing process of enlarging knowledge and understanding; and by encouraging the collaboration of his students in his research he would insure its continuation.

The philosophical faculty that Humboldt envisaged was a community of scholars. They worked independent of one other in different fields of equal importance, and they used different methods suited to their disciplines; research in each discipline had its own method. The pursuit of research by a specialized method was a precondition of a discipline's autonomy.[20]

Ranke's concept of history, which limited the task of a historian to a narration of facts but also assigned to him the task of establishing these facts by a critical method, must be seen therefore in this broader context, as part of the efforts of the time to redefine the

[20] See O. Vossler, "Humboldts Idee der Universität," *Historische Zeitschrift* 178 (1954): 251–268, and also the outline of the basic ideas behind Humboldt's university reform in Helmut Schelsky, *Einsamkeit und Freiheit* (Düsseldorf, 1977).

relation of research, learning, and education. The concordance of Ranke's view on the historian's task with this new concept of scholarship was an important factor in the quick ascent of the young history teacher to a professorship at the University of Berlin.

IV.

The separation of history from law and theology, from instruction in ethics and modern diplomacy, and the acceptance of history as an autonomous discipline left open a most important question: that of history's relation to philosophy. Beyond the general aim of searching for truth, other disciplines of the philosophical faculty—like geography, mathematics, philology, or chemistry—used research to find knowledge that could have practical applications. Knowledge of the past could hardly be considered to serve such specific purposes. What could you learn from the study of human activities in former centuries? Was the purpose of the study of the past really different from the purpose of philosophy? Was history different from philosophy? This question, which in the present situation of historical scholarship seems without much substance, was of critical importance in the age of Fichte and Hegel, when historical developments were seen as stages following a predetermined course toward the realization of ideas. When in the *Histories of the Latin and Teutonic Nations* Ranke disparaged the "poeticizing" and "fantasizing" in historical writing, he was alluding to attempts that had been made to construct history according to the demands of a philosophical system. Moreover, in various lectures that he gave in these first decades of his career he often discussed the relation between philosophy and history, and he expressed his opposition to inferring the course of the future from "a priori ideas." Ranke saw as a decisive factor in the conflict between philosophy and history the claim of the philosopher "that mankind is on an uninterrupted road to progress, in a steady development towards perfection."[21] The philosopher, starting from a truth his reason had discovered outside history, constructed a historical process that fitted his views on the destiny of humankind. Ranke emphasized that "such history would lose all autonomy," and since history would be concerned only with demonstrating the existence of a philosophical idea behind the reality of the past, there would be no interest in taking a deeper look into the past to find out how people lived and thought. In Ranke's view the subordination of history to philosophy is wrong because the approaches of history and philosophy are diametrically opposed. "There are really only two ways of acquiring knowledge about human affairs—through the perception of the particular, or through abstraction; the latter is the method of philosophy, the former of history."[22]

Ranke's refusal to accept the supremacy of philosophy over history earned him a disparaging remark by Hegel, that he was nothing but "a common historian."[23] On the other hand, this comment made Ranke welcome in the circle of anti-Hegelians—of Schleiermacher, Savigny, and Varnhagen. Ranke was aware,

[21] See *The Varieties of History*, ed. Fritz Stern (New York, 1973), 58 (from a fragment of 1830); for the original German text of this fragment, see *Aus Werk und Nachlass*, 4:72–89, particularly 86–87.

[22] *Aus Werk und Nachlass*, 4:87, and English translation in *The Varieties of History*, 58.

[23] See Ernst Simon, *Ranke und Hegel* (Munich, 1928), 82, for the origin of this remark.

however, that "pleasure in the particular," "affection
for this creature, so good and so evil, so noble and so
bestial, so cultured and so brutal, striving for eternity,
yet enslaved by the moment,"[24] was not sufficient to
claim for history the importance granted to those disciplines which enlarged knowledge of the factual and
intellectual world. Ranke emphasized that to be a
scholarly discipline history must be more than an "immense aggregate of facts." He believed that history was
"able to lift itself in is own fashion from the investigation and observation of particulars to a universal
view of events, to a knowledge of the objectively existing relatedness."[25]

Man ought not to fix his sight on a distant aim to be
accomplished in the course of world history. The
world as it exists is God's world: "In all of history lives
God, can He be recognized, every action gives evidence
of Him, every moment preaches His name."[26] The
place of a divine world government remains hidden
from man. Reason and argument could never reveal it
to him. What man *can* do is learn to see the world as
it is, and history can teach him this. Then he may not
only learn about events but at times become aware of
"the hand of God above them."[27]

V.

Establishment of the facts of history alone did not
show the world as it actually was; if you looked at

[24] *Aus Werk und Nachlass*, 4:88.

[25] Ibid., 87–88; English translation in *The Varieties of History*, p.
59.

[26] Leopold von Ranke, *Zur eigenen Lebensgeschichte*, ed. A. Dove
(Leipzig, 1890), 89.

[27] End of the preface of the *Geschichten der*, viii.

these facts and visualized their emergence, how they intertwined and became enfolded in new relationships, you might sometimes glimpse the directing power beyond the growing array of facts. This belief informed Ranke's work, determining the variety of subjects he explored and his presentation of the facts in an artistic form that enabled the reader to visualize the past. And it informed the concept that is ever-present and dominant in all his works: the concept of Europe.

In the preface of the *Histories of the Latin and Teutonic Nations* Ranke wrote that "New York and Lima are more our concern than Kiev and Smolensk."[28] This was an astounding statement, especially since Ranke wrote it only twelve years after Napoleon had invaded Russia.

This remark indicates that Ranke's idea of Europe was not identical with the geographical entity.[29] In Ranke's view not all of what constituted Europe according to the views of geographers and the general public had those qualities which gave Europe its distinction. Ranke excluded the areas that were under Turkish rule, and he also excluded Poland and Hungary from the community of European nations; their constitutions and institutions, he felt, had made no contribution to the general development, and they had not been shaped by that development's repercussions. Ranke's Europe was circumscribed not by geography but by a common spiritual experience. Europe had been formed in the days of the Völkerwanderung when the German tribes had invaded the Roman empire and when Christianity had built a bridge between inhabit-

[28] Ibid., xxx–ix.
[29] For the following see particularly ibid., xviii–xxxvii.

ants and invaders. Defense against the invasions of other nations, and, later, the common enterprise of the Crusades, strengthened the feeling that the constituent elements of the Germanic-Roman society belonged together. They were now united by another common enterprise: the extension of Europe over the oceans, and the foundation of plantations and colonies.

Ranke's concept of Europe was based on a few fundamental notions. Europe was the area that God had chosen for the birth and growth of true religion. Thus the bond that held Europe together and established it as a distinctive unit was of a spiritual nature: Christianity. The growth and strength of Christianity had represented a challenge to the structure of the Roman empire; the tension involved in the conflicting claims of state and religion and the struggles arising from them became a dominant issue in the development of European history. Because Christianity grew up in times when the Roman empire was in decline and its frontiers were overrun, its adherents could carry out their mission to spread Christianity over the entire world. But in adjusting to the different situations that existed in the various parts of Europe, Christianity accepted the simultaneous existence of diverse political formations within the larger unit of Europe, which made the problem of the relation between the individual and the general a central issue in European history.

By propounding that the factor determining the concept of Europe was not geography but a common spiritual and intellectual heritage, Ranke undermined the principle of organization which almost all his contemporaries among German historians had used in writing about European history.[30] They wrote histories of individual states as if they existed in isolation, and when they did write about Europe, they divided Europe into two groups of states, southern Europe and northern Europe, and they treated past events in these two areas as if they had little connection with each other. For Ranke Europe had gained life and existence by a spiritual development that bound the Latin and Germanic nations into an interrelated community so that whatever happened in one of these nations had repercussions in all of them. In regarding this interrelationship as crucial in constituting Europe as a reality, Ranke also established what is considered the central characteristics of his historiography and of the historical writings of his circle: its emphasis on political history.

Ranke's view of Europe embraced both a recognition of national individuality and a tendency toward unity. Conflicts arose from competition among the individual political formations, but also from conflicts that set the individual political formation against a power

[30] For a representative distinction between northern and southern Europe, see Arnold Heeren, *Handbuch der Geschichte des Europäischen Staatensystems und seiner Colonieen.* (Göttingen, 1819); Karl Friedrich Eichhorn, in his *Weltgeschichte* (Göttingen, 1817), distinguished between an unconnected Europe in earlier times and a connected Europe in more recent times, but even in his discussion of the connected Europe emphasis is placed on the isolated history of individual countries: Italy, Spain, France. Ludwig Spittler's *Entwurf der Geschichte der Europäischen Staaten* (Berlin, 1793–1974) is a history of isolated states rather than a history of a connected state system. Ranke's statement in *Geschichten der*, xxxv, "an eine Isolierung der Völker im Mittelalter, von der man so viel redet, ist hienach nicht sehr zu glauben," is a rejection of the prevailing treatment of medieval history as the history of separate states or regions.

trying to establish unity and hegemony; such conflicts were inherent in the history of Europe. This notion of Europe as a place of unavoidable conflicts explains the importance that, from his earliest writings, Ranke placed on two concepts: the notion of the great powers, and the idea of balance of power. In various of his courses in the early 1830s Ranke presented "the formation of the great powers" as an essential element of modern history.[31] He wrote that "there is no nation on earth that has not had some contact with other nations,"[32] but this relationship developed uniquely for each nation. Some nations were more powerfully armed than others, and these have come to exert a pre-eminent influence on the rest. Hence attention should be focused on those nations "that have played a pre-eminent, active role in history. We should concern ourselves with the influence which these nations have had on one another, with the struggles they have waged with one another, with their development in peace and war."

Of equal importance with the role of the great powers was Ranke's concern with the notion of balance of power. It was clearly tied to Ranke's view that although Europe was a unit it should not be centrally controlled. There is a passage in the *Histories of the Latin and Teutonic Nations* that classically exemplifies Ranke's rejection of the notion of a centrally ruled Europe. When Ranke wrote about the failure of Maximilian's plan to establish "a universal monarchy over all the German-Latin nations," he added, "God did not

[31] See *Aus Werk und Nachlass*, 4:90–91, 110.

[32] *The Varieties of History*, 59–60 for this and the following quotation; for the original German text, see *Aus Werk und Nachlass*, 4:88.

want this to happen."[33] The notion of balance of power gave some assurance against this danger. It contained two elements: first, it meant that some states are of relatively equal strength so that none can conquer all the others. But it meant also that when one state succeeds in attaining overwhelming power the others join together to thwart the pretensions of such an "exorbitant" power. Ranke continued, "In great danger one can safely trust in the guardian spirit which always protects Europe from domination by any one-sided and violent tendency, which always meets pressure on the one side with resistance on the other, and through a union of the whole which grows firmer from decade to decade, has happily preserved the freedom and separate existence of each state."[34]

VI.

When Ranke's scholarly career began, interest in history and the forms that this interest took were determined by the most recent past. For Ranke, as for most historians of his time, the French Revolution and the Napoleonic Age were decisive influences. The questions of historical continuity and revolutionary change, of the relation of rulers to ruled, of the role of the individual in history, and of the idea of the nation as supreme political principle—all central and decisive issues in the development of modern historiography—moved into the center of historical thinking under the impact of the events of the twenty-five years that followed the fall of the Bastille.[35] Like the historical out-

---

[33] *Geschichten der*, 237.

[34] I quote here from the English translation of Ranke's essay on "The Great Powers" in von Laue, Leopold Ranke, 189.

[35] See chap. I above for a more detailed discussion of the impact of the revolutionary period on historical thinking.

look of his contemporaries Ranke's thought was
shaped by this watershed. But whereas most of his
contemporaries directed their attention to the rise of
those forces which had brought about a new period of
history, Ranke saw in the events of the revolutionary
period the confirmation of Europe's basic unchange-
able nature. He thought the most important lesson
that could be drawn from the events of the preceding
decades was the survival of the great powers, the restoration of a society of states. It was the great experience of Ranke's early years that, despite the storms to
which the Revolution and Napoleon had subjected it,
Europe's basic structure had been successfully maintained.

Ranke was a conservative, a man of the Restoration,
but such a characterization should not blind us to his
signal achievement. In his writings European history
first became a reality, and this new view of modern
European history has guided historical scholarship for
more than a century.

CHAPTER III

‴|||||||||‴

RANKE AND THE MEANING
OF HISTORY

E VER SINCE Ranke's time historians have appealed
to his name and his writings in an attempt to
justify their approach to the study of the past,
but his imprint on the development of historical scholarship has been interpreted in different ways. He is
thought to be the advocate and defender of two contradictory claims about the purposes of historical scholarship.

One claim is that history is a science, that it is primarily concerned with facts and their causal connection—how they acted upon each other. The historian
works with materials contemporary with the time on
which he focuses, or at least with early reports about
the past, preferably documents, whose exactitude and
reliability have to be subjected to critical examination.
Like any other science, therefore, history has its own
method, the critical method, and Ranke is understood
to have extended the critical method of philology to
the entire study of the past. Research in the sources of
the past, using the critical method, became the precondition and the center of historical scholarship. According to this view, Ranke is to be praised as the origina-
tor of scientific history.

But Ranke's work has also been differently interpreted. Despite his own assertions about the relation

between history and philosophy, which I have discussed in chapter II, he is said to have integrated into the study of the past the notions of German idealistic philosophy. Here the view is that there are forces at work in human existence and social life whereby ideas attain realization; and the task of the historian is to show the relationship of the struggles of the past to the ideas that stood behind them. Thus the historian has not only to set forth the story of past events but to reach for what is behind them—their meaning. In assigning history this task, Ranke, it has been said, followed Wilhelm von Humboldt, who in his famous treatise on the task of the historian had written: "One has scarcely arrived at the skeleton of an event by a crude sorting out of what actually happened. What is so achieved is the necessary basis of history, its raw material, but not history itself. To stop here would be to sacrifice the actual inner truth, well founded within the causal nexus, for an outward, literal, and seeming truth."[1]

It is striking that those who regard Ranke as the advocate of scientific history, as well as those who consider him to be the representative of German idealistic philosophy, find justification for their view of Ranke's message in the same statement: the famous, so frequently quoted sentence from the preface of Ranke's first book, the *Histories of the Latin and Teutonic Nations*, in which Ranke writes that he only wants to say "wie es eigentlich gewesen."[2]

[1] An English translation of Wilhelm von Humboldt's famous essay "Über die Aufgabe des Geschichtsschreibers" will be found in *History and Theory* 6 (1967): 57–71.

[2] *Geschichten der romanischen und germanischen Völker von*

I quote this statement in German; its translation into English has its problems, as is attested by the variety of renderings that have been offered. The difficulty lies in the ambivalence of the word *eigentlich*. Does Ranke say that he has limited himself to showing how it "essentially" was, how it "really" was, how it "actually" was? These are the expressions that have been used to translate the word *eigentlich* into English. *Essentially*, and to a certain extent also *really*, seem to refer to a truth that lies beneath the surface of facts; the historian must penetrate this surface to get at the essence of events. On the other hand, translating *eigentlich* as "the actual past" or "actually" suggests that the final aim of the historian is the precise rendering of facts. The term *eigentlich* is of such an opaque character that all these translations seem possible. Thus the exact meaning of the statement seems uncertain, and this explains why the same statement could serve different, contradictory interpretations.

Can we establish what Ranke really meant? The statement has been quoted innumerable times—with or without attribution to Ranke—but it is usually quoted out of context. It might be worthwhile, therefore, to see whether the remark remains ambivalent, if not self-contradictory, when it is set back again into its context.

The famous phrase "wie es eigentlich gewesen" follows the statement that history has been assigned the function of judging the past, of instructing men for the profit of future years. Ranke, as he goes on to say, does

---

1494 bis 1535 (Leipzig, 1824), 1:vi; see also chap. II above for a discussion of the implications of this statement.

not aspire to such lofty undertakings; he only wants to report "wie es eigentlich gewesen." Although Ranke's disavowal of using his historical investigation to teach morals or politics sounds modest, it is not meant to assign to the historian an inferior position. Those who read this passage when Ranke's book appeared in 1824 cannot have believed that these were purely theoretical observations. They must have been aware that the remarks had a polemical character, that they aimed at special targets and implied a rejection of widely held beliefs.

One of the widely held views that Ranke attacked was that history showed the need for strict obedience to moral laws—the central theme of the most popular and most widely read German historian, F. C. Schlosser, whose *World History*[3] was published at the time Ranke was writing his preface. Another notion Ranke rejected stemmed from Machiavelli's historically based political doctrines, which had been widely discussed in Germany at the end of the eighteenth century. In his analysis of Machiavelli's *Discorsi* later in the book,[4] Ranke states that Machiavelli is not concerned with an explanation and understanding of the past, but only with the establishment of rules valid for the future. In repudiating both these views, Ranke takes a stand against prevalent notions about the use of history. Ranke implies that whenever a historian uses the past to present his views about how people ought to behave and act, the picture of the past becomes distorted and false. The historian ought not to

[3] Friedrich Christoph Schlosser, *Weltgeschichte in zusammen-hängender Darstellung*, published in Frankfurt from 1816 to 1824.

[4] In the supplementary volume of the *Geschichten der* entitled *Zur Kritik neuerer Geschichtschreiber*, 189.

go beyond the limits of his task: to show how things were in fact.

There is further proof in the preface that this statement ought to be understood in its limited, literal sense, that it was not meant to be a pronouncement about the meaning of history—proof that, in my opinion, most incomprehensibly has been overlooked. Three paragraphs further on, Ranke makes another statement about his aims, a statement I also cited above in chapter II that certainly does not support the philosophical and programmatic interpretations given to the phrase "wie es eigentlich gewesen." In moving words, Ranke relates his conviction that it is not up to man to know and to explain the course of world history and that such a goal is beyond the human reach. "One tries, one strives, but in the end it is not attained. Let none be disheartened by this. The most important thing is always what we deal with. . . . humanity as it is, explicable or inexplicable: the life of the individual, of generations, and of nations, and at times the hand of God above them."[5]

By suggesting that Ranke's statement did not imply more than what it said—in reducing it to its literal meaning—I do not mean to say that it is insignificant. On the contrary, in its literal meaning it directs attention to an aspect of Ranke's achievement that has been frequently slighted, if not disregarded. I refer to the lit-

[5] *Geschichten der,* viii: "Man bemüht sich, man strebt, am Ende hat man's nicht erreicht. Dass nur niemand darüber ungeduldig werde! Die Hauptsache ist immer, wovon wir handeln. . . . Menschheit wie sie ist, erklärlich oder unerklärlich: das Leben des Einzelnen, der Geschlechter, der Völker, zuweilen die Hand Gottes über ihnen."

erary aspects of Ranke's work: specifically, his view that history is a part of literature. Showing the past as it had actually been meant not only establishing the facts as correctly as possible, but also placing them in their contemporary context in such a way that the past would come to life again.

For Ranke, a historian must be not only a critical investigator but also a writer.[6] Ranke grew up in the classical age of German literature. His journals and notes show his admiration for Goethe and his steady interest in Goethe's works. For Ranke, as for many of his contemporaries, the novels of Walter Scott had been an important stimulus that awakened his interest in the events of former times, even though he was upset by the erroneous statements he found in them. He had no doubt that historical books were—or ought to be—works of literature. One confirmation of Ranke's concern with the literary qualities of his work is a revision he made in later editions of his work: his desire to *say* ("sagen") became a desire to *show* ("zeigen") "wie es eigentlich gewesen."[7]

Because so little attention has been given to this implication of Ranke's statement, and because studies of Ranke are strangely lacking in appreciations of his literary art, our interpretation of its meaning might be appropriately supplemented by an examination, from

[6] Regarding the emphasis that Ranke placed on "history as art," see chap. II above.

[7] See Michael-Joachim Zemlin, *Geschichte zwischen Theorie und Theoria-Untersuchungen zur Geschichtsphilosophie Rankes* (Würzburg, 1988), particularly chap. 4, sec. 3, although the author seems to me to ascribe too much importance to the change from "sagen" to "zeigen."

the literary point of view, of the book on which Ranke worked throughout the decade following the publication of the *Histories of the Latin and Teutonic Nations* and which is usually regarded as his first great masterwork, *The History of the Popes*.[8]

As far as possible Ranke, in this work, avoids summary statements and lets the narrator disappear from the story so that the reader is directly confronted with facts and events. Ranke wants the reader to experience the story as a participant. The use of literary techniques enables Ranke to diminish the distance that separates past from present, to give the story a pattern that alternates between description of situations and of actions, and, above all, to make the work conform to the primary requisite of a literary work: to tell a story that is full of tension.

In order to make the reader aware that the past is not fundamentally different from the present, Ranke points out the continuities between past and present. Most of his readers, he assumes, live "on this side of the Alps,"[9] and he reminds them that life on the other side is even now somewhat different from that lived in northern Europe. Nevertheless much is the same. As at present, Italy in the sixteenth century was dominated by foreign powers; Ferrara was as "desolate and deserted"[10] as it is now; Venice had its "beautiful

[8] The original German title was *Die Römischen Päpste, ihre Kirche und ihr Staat im XVI. und XVII. Jahrhundert*; the work was published in the years 1834–1836. In the following I shall base my quotations on the text printed in Leopold von Ranke, *Sämmtliche Werke* (Leipzig, 1878), vols. 37–39.

[9] *Sämmtliche Werke*, 37:112.

[10] Ibid., 38:169.

blondes" for whom it is still famous.[11] Then as now, Italians tried to regain courage when something went wrong by saying, "Oh, patienza."[12]

Travelers from Protestant Europe are drawn to Catholic Rome, Ranke writes, because it is "adorned with matchless works of art."[13] Ranke arouses the reader's memory of Rome by making *The History of the Popes* a kind of guidebook: he explains the origin of Rome's most famous palaces and villas, like the Palazzo Farnese and the Villa Farnesina; he describes in technical detail the erection of one of Rome's landmarks, the obelisk on the square before Saint Peter's; an entire section of the work is devoted to the building projects of Sixtus V, which gave the city its present vista.[14] On the other hand, Ranke does not conceal that Rome also saw the beginning of what he and, he assumed, his contemporaries find repellent in modern architecture: its monotonous uniformity.

In Ranke's pages, people did not behave in the past very differently from the way they do now. When Pope Pius V encountered contradiction, he became "red in the face."[15] When Gregory XIII was annoyed, he slapped the arms of his chair.[16] Pope Clement VIII was an indefatigable worker, as is shown by the detailed account that Ranke gives of his daily working schedule, and Ranke adds that he did daily health exer-

[11] Ibid., 220.
[12] Ibid., 37:209.
[13] Ibid., 69.
[14] Ibid., 307–315.
[15] Ibid., 232.
[16] Ibid.

cises.[17] Ranke does not simply state that a person was cruel or false; he demonstrates the brutality with which the Carafa pope treated those who had offended him by telling the story of the humiliation he meted out to his niece, the young Marchesa Montebello, whose husband had been one of the pope's opponents. When she returned from Naples to Rome, she found her Roman palace locked. No inn was willing to receive her; on a rainy night she drove from one to another until she was finally given shelter by an innkeeper who lived so far distant from the city that he had not received the papal orders.[18] Another example is the story through which Ranke indicates a change of the intellectual climate in the late sixteenth century. He writes that Aldus Manutius found "no admirers for his Greek or Latin; at the hour of his lectures, he might be seen pacing up and down before the portal of the university, with one or two hearers, the only persons in whom he found congeniality of sentiment or pursuit."[19]

In accord with his reluctance to make judgments or abstract statements is his hesitancy to blame the character of the people with whom his book deals. He condemns the Borgia pope whose lascivious passions he believed met general censure. In general, however, he is less concerned with the virtues and vices of the popes than with the effects of their actions. His treatment of Pope Clement VII is an example. His character could not be faulted, but because of his political errors he was the "most disastrous of all popes."[20] The man-

[17] Ibid., 38:155–156.
[18] Ibid., 37:197.
[19] Ibid., 315.
[20] Ibid., 82.

ner in which Ranke presents his story is meant to allow the reader to build up his own picture of a person's character—as in a novel in which the good and bad sides of an individual emerge only gradually.

A remarkable display of his literary art is the manner in which Ranke, through varied treatments of similar events, throws light on their changing importance. The conclaves of the earlier part of the sixteenth century are mentioned only very briefly; however, the qualities of the various cardinals, the negotiations that went on during the conclaves, and finally their outcome are extensively discussed in Ranke's treatment of the conclaves of the later sixteenth century, when the popes had begun to exert a steadily increasing influence on European politics. Ranke handles the distribution of space in a deliberate, but also majestic, manner. For instance, *The History of the Popes* contains a remarkably detailed report about a battle that decided what Ranke called "a little war," whereas only one paragraph, barely more than a single sentence, is devoted to the destruction of the Armada. There are reasons for this. The battle in the "little war" was fought with the methods and in the spirit of the Italian wars of the period from 1494 to 1531. It signified the end of this kind of warfare, and against this detailed description the changes in military techniques and in the conduct of war in the following period stand out sharply and clearly. Little space is given to the defeat of the Armada because it is only an episode in a conflict that had started earlier and that continued, so that, despite its sensational character, the defeat of the Armada was not decisive and could not be considered to have brought about a change in the political scene. Whenever an event represented a turning point, it receives extended treatment. Although the account of diplomatic negotiations is usually restricted to a brief summary of their results, the report about the negotiations that led to the absolution of Henry IV follows them carefully through all their stages. The long and detailed description that they receive indicates that these negotiations represented a decisive event in the religious struggle.

Because for Ranke a historical work was a work of literature, it had to be a story with a beginning and an end—it had to have, in other words, structure. *The History of the Popes* is not strictly a chronologically organized book. It is a work wound around one great theme: the relationship between state and church in Europe. At the outset Ranke writes that the rise of Christianity involved separation of Church and State, and that this was the "greatest, perhaps the most consequential characteristic of Christian times."[21] From then on, the development of the relationship of these two powers becomes the dominating issue in European history. Originally the Church had been dependent on the State, but its need for independence required the creation of a secular church-state; in consequence, the Church became involved in secular as well as in spiritual affairs. The history of the modern papacy—that is, the history that Ranke wrote—began when the secular and the spiritual interests of the papacy came in conflict with each other and when, simultaneously, the secularization of the Church led to a spiritual opposition within the Church. In the first three books of his work, Ranke lays out the tensions

[21] Ibid., 8.

that resulted from these involvements and interrela-
tionships. This first part of the story reaches its con-
clusion when the worldly power of the Church became
consolidated, but also reduced to a relatively small
area, so that the inner contradictions that had beset papal policy were eliminated and papal policy became
subordinated to the reestablishment of the Church's
unity.

The remainder of the book describes the progress
that the papacy made in reestablishing the authority
of the Church in Europe. But it also shows that the
success of the papacy reawakened the old tensions on
a new level. In its fight against those who defected
from the Church, the papacy had to rely on secular allies; in consequence, among its allies the fear arose
that they would become subordinate to the chief political protector of the papacy, the Habsburgs. The popes
themselves became fearful of the reemergence of the
medieval situation, in which the popes had been dependent on the power of the emperor. Thus, at the
time when victory seemed imminent, the Catholic
camp lost its inner unity. Some of its members supported the Protestants—for instance, France, which fa-
vored the entry of Sweden into the war against the
Habsburgs—and the pope himself encouraged some resistance against the further extension of imperial
power: "Catholicism seen as a unit could not stand its
own victories."[22] Thus, the conflict between secular
and spiritual power, after having reached its high point
and its crisis in the 150 years between the beginning
of the sixteenth century and the middle of the seven-

[22] Ibid., 38:371.

teenth century, ended in the establishment of a number of independent states, each of which gave to the relationship of its political and religious institutions its own form. "It cannot be imagined any longer that one or the other confession might be raised to universal rule. What is important is that all peoples, every state, can develop their forces on the basis of their political-religious convictions. That is the foundation of the future world."[23]

Ranke does not name a power that directs the course of events, but he does mention a variety of forces as causing the developments of history. He suggests that there is a "plan of a divine world government,"[24] that all human doings are subject to a "quiet and almost unnoticeable but powerful and irresistible force,"[25] that there is "necessity in events."[26] Ranke also indicates that ideas might be the moving forces.[27] The individual, as insignificant as he appears in the face of world history, is able to develop unexpected strength in the face of disaster. All that can be said is that there is constant movement in life. Those involved in the events and struggles of their time cannot know what the outcome will be or where events will lead.[28] But that also gives the study of history its significance and value. Only retrospection reveals the design in the events of world history. "Every action of the past gives

23 Ibid., 377.
24 Ibid., 37:22.
25 Ibid., 177.
26 Ibid., 38:161.
27 Ibid., 235.
28 Ibid., 37:177.

evidence of God, every moment preaches His name."[29] The study of the past has a much greater aim than the teaching of morals or instruction in the conduct of politics. There is a priestly dignity in the historian's task to show "wie es eigentlich gewesen."

[29] Leopold von Ranke, *Das Briefwerk*, ed. W. P. Fuchs (Hamburg, 1949), 18.

CHAPTER IV

''''''''||||||''''''

BURCKHARDT'S CONCEPT OF
CULTURAL HISTORY

I.

WHEN HIS YEARS of study came to an end, Jacob Burckhardt decided to work in a particular field of history: in cultural history.[1] What did that decision mean? What did he understand by this term? Did his conception of cultural history undergo significant changes in the course of his life? These are the questions with which this chapter is concerned.

In the early 1840s, cultural history was a small but recognized special field. Karl Dietrich Hüllmann was one of the few professors who offered lectures on cultural history, and he has left a description of what he considered cultural history to be: "So far," he stated, "history has always been treated in a very one-sided way; it has been exclusively concerned with those who have been influential and have written about their experiences. Scant attention has been paid to the lower classes [Niedere Volk] or to the age in general. This is the aim of cultural history, which, without regard to social status or to language, encompasses the whole of humanity. It illustrates the outstanding stages of development through which the prominent

[1] See my article, "Jacob Burckhardt's Student Years," *Journal of the History of Ideas* 47 (1986): 249–274.

nations of the whole world have passed till they have reached the situation in which they are now."[2]

This statement assigns to cultural history two related but distinctive functions. First of all cultural history has the task of recording the daily life of society and of all its groups. Indeed, in the six volumes in which Hüllmann described life in the towns of the Middle Ages,[3] he dealt with the most varied aspects of urban life: guild regulations and festivities, drinking habits and gambling, the relation of dress to social standing, family life and prostitution—all aspects of what we would now call social history. It is no accident that Hüllmann's work in cultural history was centered on urban life. Towns were a favorite subject of cultural historians, and the connection between cultural history and towns had come to exist as the very words *culture* and *cultural* gained currency.[4] These words had appeared in the German language only at the end of the eighteenth century and were then meant to signify the effort and the result of imposing reason and system on human activities. In this process of "cultivation" the development of towns was considered to have been of decisive importance; they were the focus of intense economic activity and they also

---

[2] This quotation comes from notes taken by a student in Hüllmann's lectures on cultural history, preserved among Hüllmann's papers in the Bonn University Archives. Hüllman was a professor in Bonn and, when Burckhardt studied there, presented a course on the cultural history of the Middle Ages.

[3] Hüllmann, *Städtewesen des Mittelalters* (Bonn, 1826–1827).

[4] For the development of the concept of "culture," see J. Niedermann, *Kultur: Werden und Wandlungen des Begriffs von Cicero bis Herder* (Florence, 1941). The treatment of "cultural history" in German works on the history of historiography is not satisfactory.

stimulated intellectual life. At the end of the eighteenth century and the beginning of the nineteenth, the history of towns had a particular, almost personal interest to German academics. Towns had given rise to the middle classes and academics usually came from those classes, which were then struggling for a greater role in government and civic affairs.

According to Hüllmann's statement cultural history had a further purpose: to distinguish epochs of history from each other and to describe the stages of development through which the leading nations of the world had passed. One reason this function was ascribed to cultural history was the great popularity that the notion of *Zeitgeist* had acquired in the eighteenth century; those living in this enlightened age felt different from, and superior to, other periods of history. Voltaire had spread widely this view of the qualitative difference of historical periods with his distinction of "four brilliant ages" that stand out from the course of history: the times of Alexander and Pericles, of Caesar and Augustus, of the Medici, and of the "siècle de Louis XIV." Clearly, this kind of cultural history shifted emphasis to the preeminent classes of society, to literature and art, and to education and scholarly activities.

In the early years of his scholarly career, when Burckhardt referred to cultural history, his notions were similar to those of Hüllmann and other cultural historians of that time. Burckhardt's dissertation on Konrad von Hochstaden, published in 1843, contains detailed descriptions of social life. When in 1848—after six somewhat restless years in Berlin, Basel, and Italy—Burckhardt decided to accept a position in Basel

as teacher of history at the university and at the Päda-
gogium, he came with a plan to edit a library of cultural history.[5] It was to consist of a number of small,
relatively cheap volumes aimed at the general public.
Burckhardt's plan gives the titles of the prospective
volumes: *The Age of Pericles, The Times of the Later
Roman Emperors, The Century of Charlemagne, The
Period of the Hohenstaufen, German Life in the Fifteenth Century, The Age of Raphael*. The criterion
Burckhardt used for giving each volume a special
theme was the cultural distinctiveness and coherence
of an epoch. An example of what Burckhardt expected
these volumes to contain is revealed in a course of lectures he gave in Basel in the winter of 1849/50,[6] which

  [5] This plan is outlined in Burckhardt's letter to Andreas Heusler-
Rybiner dated July 19, 1848, in *Briefe* (Basel, 1949–1980), 3:94.
Werner Kaegi, in his *Jacob Burckhardt Eine Biographie* (Basel,
1947–1982), 3:169–176, calls this project a "Lebensplan." Peter
Ganz, in his article, "Jacob Burckhardts *Kultur der Renaissance in
Italien*: Handwerk und Methode," *Deutsche Vierteljahrsschrift für
Literaturwissenschaft und Geistesgeschichte* (1988): 25, states that
Burckhardt's *Age of Constantine* and *Civilization of the Renaissance in Italy* were the beginning and ending of a plan to publish a
series of studies of cultural history dealing with the Middle Ages. I
believe that too much emphasis ought not to be placed on the connection between Burckhardt's later writings and the project discussed in his letter to Heusler-Rybiner. The letter to Friedrich von
Preen, May 31, 1874, in *Briefe*, 5:225, in which Burckhardt refers
to the project of 1848, reveals that he himself felt that there was a
clear break between his scholarly activities before and after the
early fifties. This chapter shows that in the *Constantine*, and still
more in *The Civilization of the Renaissance in Italy*, the experiences of the years after 1848 were crucial.

  [6] Kaegi discusses these lectures in his *Jacob Burkhardt*, 3:326–
350. However, although his letters show the centrality that the
study of the Middle Ages had in the early years of Burckhardt's his-

fell under the rubric of "The Heyday of the Middle Ages" and treated the European Middle Ages from the eleventh to the fourteenth century as a coherent and unified period, distinctly separated from the preceding and the following centuries. At the outset of this course of lectures Burckhardt made it clear that he did not intend to discuss political developments, chronology, and geography. Rather he would lecture on medieval life in its relation to the spiritual trends that were at work throughout the entire period and created a common attitude in the various European nations. Evidently Burckhardt intended to combine a description of the varieties of life with an analysis of the all-pervasive, unique character of the period. In the course of these lectures Burckhardt discussed the organization and the impact of the Church, the rise of the towns, and the origin of the mendicant orders, and he offered an appraisal of what he called the greatest artistic achievement of the Middle Ages, the Gothic cathedral. But his lectures were primarily concerned with the dominant social class of that time: the knights. Burckhardt regarded them as crucially important because their ideals permeated the period, inspiring a sense of honor that the ancient world had not known, and creating the conditions for the emergence of knightly epic and poetry.

We do not know whether this picture of the culture of the High Middle Ages was meant to be a model of what the single volumes of Burckhardt's projected library were to contain, or whether, in these lectures, he

---

torical scholarship, they seem to me no proof that the Middle Ages continued to have crucial importance in his historical thought.

made use of material he had collected for a particular volume in this series that was now no longer needed for this purpose. Soon after Burckhardt settled in Basel, he abandoned his plan for a library of cultural history.

II.

Burckhardt turned to another subject: in 1852 *The Age of Constantine the Great* appeared, the first of Burckhardt's three cultural histories. *The Age of Constantine* was followed by *The Civilization of the Renaissance in Italy* in 1860, and by the *Greek Cultural History* in 1898. *The Age of Constantine* has particular importance for the development of Burckhardt's concept of cultural history. When he began writing it, he intended it to conform to the prevailing notions of this genre. As he worked his way into the topic he found himself increasingly restricted by these notions. He began, then, to examine them critically and to chart his own course.

Not until twenty-eight years after its first appearance, in the preface to the second edition of the *Constantine*, did Burckhardt call this work a cultural history;[7] such a characterization is not to be found in the text of the book. At the time of its first publication in 1853, Burckhardt made remarks which suggest that he had intended to write a cultural history but that he had encountered difficulties. His aim had been to "bring together the significant characteristic aspects of the world of that time in a vivid picture," that is, to achieve what was regarded as the particular task of

[7] "kulturhistorische Gesamtschilderung." This second preface is printed in *Jacob Burckhardt Gesamtausgabe* (Stuttgart, 1930–1933), 2:3; the preface to the first edition is printed on pp. 1–2.

cultural history. However, he continued, he had not been able to carry out this plan because wide areas of the life of that time, particularly its economic and financial aspects, had not yet been sufficiently explored. However, a letter written at about the same time[8] indicates that this was hardly the main reason for what Burckhardt then called the "unevenness of the book." The difficulty he had encountered was to fit into the existing framework of cultural history an evaluation of the contribution that a particular period had made to the development of world history.

In writing *The Age of Constantine* Burckhardt became aware that it was not possible to treat a period of the past as a separate or independent unit. The historian is interested in the past because of its bearing upon the present, and the contribution of a past period to the course of world history must form an integral element of every evaluation of the past. Awareness of the interrelationship between past and present became a crucial element in Burckhardt's concept of cultural history. *Constantine* is the first expression of what became a fundamental characteristic of his approach to the past.

For a young scholar who had worked on German medieval history and on art history, the choice of the Age of Constantine as a subject of extended historical research is astonishing and deserves some attention. It seems likely, almost certain, that Burckhardt received the first impulse for the *Constantine* in the summer semester of 1841, when he studied in Bonn. There he was a member of the group around Gottfried Kinkel, and he became Kinkel's particular friend. One of Kin-

[8] Letter to Hottinger, December 2, 1852, in *Briefe*, 3:170–171.

kel's most popular lecture courses at the university was "The History of Paganism." This course represented the outline of a book in which Kinkel intended to write about the first three centuries after the birth of Christ, analyzing the political and intellectual developments in the course of which the victory of Christianity became a "historical necessity."[9] After Burckhardt had left Bonn, Kinkel's plans for this book were often mentioned in the correspondence between the two men.[10] Burckhardt seems to have concentrated fully on *The Age of Constantine* only after it had become clear to him that Kinkel would never write a book on this topic.

The dominating issue of *The Age of Constantine*—the victory of Christianity over paganism—had interest and significance because it seemed a mirror image of the recent German past, when a new attitude toward life and ethics based on philosophy and neoclassicism was undermining the validity of traditional church doctrines. The times when the old gods were sinking had a seductive attraction in a time when they were rising again. Moreover, Burckhardt was personally involved in the debate about the relevance of the doctrines and teachings of the Protestant church. A descendant of a long line of Protestant ministers, Burckhardt was expected to follow in their footsteps and had indeed begun to study theology. He had lost his faith, however, and changed to the study of history. But among those with whom he had studied—in Switzerland, in Berlin, and Bonn—were several theologians,

[9] Gottfried Kinkel, *Selbstbiographie 1838–1848*, ed. Richard Sander (Bonn, 1931), 29.

[10] *Briefe*, 1:202, 226, 234.

and the role of Christianity in the modern world remained vital in discussions with his friends.

When Burckhardt was a student in Bonn this issue did not remain on a theoretical level. It created a serious conflict in which Kinkel was the chief figure. Kinkel too had started out as a theologian. He was a lecturer in the theological faculty of Bonn University, gave religious instruction in a school in Bonn, and preached in a Cologne parish. But Kinkel became attached to a married woman, who although seeking a divorce was still legally married, thus arousing strong disapproval in Protestant circles. Kinkel was forced to give up preaching and teaching school and, with some difficulties, he moved from the theological to the philosophical faculty of Bonn University. Not surprisingly, Kinkel turned away from Christianity and adopted a pantheistic outlook. Burckhardt watched closely as this drama unfolded. It must have been a concrete demonstration of the pressure that society, institutions, and political power could exert on an individual's personal life and religious beliefs. It gave some reality to what had happened in the times of Constantine.

Events of the recent past seemed to throw further light on the period of Constantine. Burckhardt's book is called *The Age of Constantine the Great*, a title that underlines its thesis of the overwhelming impact which a powerful personality can have on the course of history. In Burckhardt's book the victory of Christianity and the transformation of the Roman Empire from paganism to Christianity are presented as the work of one great individual, Constantine. Behind Burckhardt's belief in Constantine's ability to shape the course of history stood the figure who dominated

Burckhardt's own time: Napoleon. In reporting about Constantine's campaign against Maxentius, Burckhardt compared it to "the Italian campaign of the youthful Napoleon with which it has more than one battlefield in common,"[11] and a reference to Napoleon occurs again when Burckhardt sums up his picture of Constantine as "a genius in stature who knew no moral scruple in politics and regarded the religious question exclusively from the point of view of political expediency."[12]

Two of Burckhardt's teachers at the University of Berlin had frequently lectured on periods of transition in which two civilizations clashed. Johann Gustav Droysen had coined the term "Hellenism" to characterize the new civilization that arose from the establishment of Greek rule in Asia Minor and Egypt. And for Ranke the invasion of the German tribes into the Latin world of the Roman Empire signified the beginning of a new historical period, that of European history. In scrutinizing the process by which the victory of Christianity was attained in the Roman world, Burckhardt investigated a historical moment to which Ranke assigned crucial importance for the development of European history.

When Burckhardt wrote about the importance of Constantine he stated: "It is a remarkable concatenation of deeds and destiny to which ambitious men who are highly gifted are drawn as by some mysterious power." The Great Man acts by the principle of "necessity." While he "believes that he himself is ruling

---

[11] The English quotations of Burckhardt's *Age of Constantine the Great* are taken from the translation by Moses Hadas (New York, 1949), 270.

[12] Ibid., 283.

his age and determining its character," in reality "an epoch is expressed in his person"—that is why he is able to determine and change the course of history.[13]

This view of the historical significance of a great personality hardly permits the presentation of a past era in accordance with the prevailing notions of cultural history. The world of action and the world of daily life seem far apart. Descriptions of a static character, which cultural history demanded, could not explain why this was a period of transition in which a decisive change in world history took place.

Nevertheless, Burckhardt's concern with fulfilling the demands of conventional cultural history is very noticeable in the *Constantine*. Burckhardt describes in detail the differences in the habits and behavior of the Gauls, the Britons, and the Germans, thereby directing attention to the problems involved in maintaining control over an empire of such varied composition. Cultural differences emerge sharply in Burckhardt's characterization of the great metropolitan centers: Alexandria, "which no other city of the world could equal in splendor in material as well as spiritual activities but also in corruption," and Rome, with both a refined Christian and pagan high society and masses craving for spectacles. Some of the most interesting passages of the book deal with life in the caves and huts to which the first eremites retired; the reader is made aware of the existence of strains and attitudes that came to full development in medieval Christianity. Because of these descriptions of situations in the various parts of the empire, the book has a remarkable liveliness.

[13] Ibid., 262.

By describing individual situations with concreteness and precision Burckhardt showed his intent to fit his work into the accepted pattern of cultural history, but it lacks, as Burckhardt himself remarked, "a consistent principle of presentation."[14] There was a marked difference between the detailed account of a static situation and the explanation of the dynamic development that made the age of Constantine a crucial factor in the formation of modern Europe.

III.

If the importance of Constantine's age for the course of world history left only limited space, as Burckhardt himself admitted, for depicting those aspects of life which were regarded as the chief topic of a cultural history, the second and most famous of Burckhardt's cultural historical works, *The Civilization of the Renaissance in Italy*, might be considered a model of what the task of a cultural historian was believed to be. It provided the picture of a particular period of the past, of a geographically and chronologically separate section of European history. The Renaissance stands by itself like a painting on an easel.

Burckhardt was most anxious to demonstrate the unity and coherence of this period, and he used a number of literary devices to create this impression. *The Civilization of the Renaissance in Italy* contains in striking frequency references to preceding or following passages. In some cases a bracketed page number appears in the text, in others a short statement like "as has been discussed above."[15] About a hundred such in-

---

[14] In the letter to Hottinger mentioned above, n. 8.

[15] Peter Ganz, "Jacob Burckhardts *Kultur der Renaissance in*

ternal references can be found in the 406 pages of the
book. Their net effect is to direct the reader's attention
to the inner connection among the varied activities of
the period, which are shown to be expressions of the
same spirit. Thus, the book is not organized chronologically but divided into sections, each of which is devoted to a different aspect of human concerns. The
topic of each section is briefly explained or summa-
rized at its outset, and these statements are then elu-
cidated by concrete examples; thus the book becomes
a series of brilliant historical vignettes. Four pages nar-
rating the rise and fall of the Baglioni in Perugia illus-
trate the ruthless practices and the perils of tyrannical
rule. We learn about the many uncertainties in the life
of a humanist from a report on a humanist's career
given in Valeriano's *De infelicitate literatorum*. A description of Pius II's tireless travels to classical ruins
brings to life the Renaissance enthusiasm for antiquity
and antiquities. However, the book does not disinte-
grate into a series of disparate pictures. In Burckhardt's
view the Renaissance was dominated by one central
notion: awareness of individuality, emphasis on "the
individual," is the novel and distinguishing feature of
the Renaissance.

Italien," 55, has also directed attention to the "Querverweise" in
the book. Ganz's article is an important study of Burckhardt's procedure in composing his picture of the Renaissance, and it throws
light on Burckhardt's scholarly method. My observations on Burckhardt's *Civilization of the Renaissance in Italy* go in a somewhat
different direction, as they are concerned with the personal experiences that were decisive in forming Burckhardt's picture of the Renaissance, and with the relation of the work to the general development of cultural history.

Although *The Civilization of the Renaissance in Italy* is a cultural history, the book begins with a political survey. Burckhardt considered the collapse of the medieval empire to be the precondition for the development of individuality. The weakening and disappearance of the power of the empire, supposed to be the controlling factor of Christian Europe, made possible the rise of small, factually autonomous political units. Within these new formations the individual found wider possibilities for movement and for social ascent; he became involved in a variety of political, economic, and intellectual activities, and was able to attain a position appropriate to his talents. The time of independent city-republics ended when the absolute monarchies of France and Spain gained control over Italy, and the possibilities for individual activity, therefore, became restricted again. These historical facts gave the period with which Burckhardt was dealing its strict chronological limits: the Renaissance began in the fourteenth century and ended in the middle of the sixteenth.

Burckhardt's book is a description of the transformation brought about by the new awareness of individuality—of the changes in attitudes, concerns, and forms of social life determined by the discovery of "the individual." Thus, Burckhardt's discussion of the political preconditions of these developments is followed by three famous sections dealing with the discovery of new human capacities consequent upon the awareness of individuality: a new idea of what man is and is able to do, the roots of this new image of man in the world of antiquity, and a shift from absorption in the world above to concern with the world below. In consequence, in this period man's interests widen and ex-

tend in new directions. He places emphasis on origi-
nality and virtuosity, he becomes curious about nature
and its working, and he cultivates capacities that lead
to success and fame in his own time. Thus changes in
social structure and social behavior, in moral assump-
tions and philosophical beliefs, in intellectual aims
and in the function of literature and art, form the contents of Burckhardt's book, but all these topics, as different and disparate as they are, are connected because
of their common origin in the discovery of "the individual."

It has frequently been considered as the main thesis
of Burckhardt's book that the revival of antiquity was
the driving force in the emergence of the new era of
the Renaissance. And, indeed, the section on the revival of antiquity stands out because it introduces an
element of movement into a primarily descriptive
work—it presents the story of a development. Yet
Burckhardt himself never regarded this section as being of central importance. He even doubted that "Renaissance" was an appropriate term to characterize the
period. In his view the changes that took place would
have taken place under any circumstances, whatever
the influence of classical literature and art had meant
for the manner in which new attitudes and beliefs
were expressed and justified.[16]

Burckhardt's *Civilization of the Renaissance* em-

---

[16] See the introduction to the third section, "The Revival of Antiquity." "Auf diesem Punkte unserer kulturgeschichtlichen Über-
sicht angelangt, müssen wir des Altertums gedenken, dessen
"Wiedergeburt" in einseitiger Weise zum Gesamtnamen des Zeit-
raums überhaupt geworden ist. Die bisher geschilderten Zustände
würden die Nation erschüttert und gereift haben auch ohne das Al-
tertum."

bodies the notions that in the first decades of the nine-teenth century were connected with the term "cul-tural history." How was it that with this work he did not encounter the difficulties which had made it im-possible to realize the prevailing notion of cultural his-tory in the *Constantine*?

In the *Constantine* the presentation of a somewhat static picture had been difficult, one might say unreal-istic, because the Age of Constantine was an epoch of crucial change in world history. The turn that history would take was an open issue: it depended on struggles between religious movements, on the shifting weight among the peoples that formed part of the empire, and, most of all, on the aims and strength of the personali-ties who were leaders in these struggles. In contrast, *The Civilization of the Renaissance in Italy* did not deal with a struggle whose outcome was hanging in the balance. The outcome had been decided. The exis-tence of the Renaissance indicated not that the direc-tion of world history's course was still uncertain, but that a world-historical change had taken place. The Renaissance bore all the characteristics of a new epoch and was presented by Burckhardt as the embodiment of the modern age.[17] The Florence of the Renaissance was "the first modern state." Modern politics formed the basis "for the early development of the Italian into a modern man, for his being the firstborn among the sons of modern Europe." Dante was "the first who in the full sense of the word became an artist because he brought imperishable contents into an imperishable

[17] I have counted some thirty passages in which Burckhardt iden-tifies the Italy of the Renaissance with the modern age, and the in-dividual Italian with "modern man."

form." The concluding statement of the work states quite categorically, "The Italian Renaissance must be called the leader of modern ages."

What does the identification of the Renaissance with the modern age—with "our time"—imply? It meant that a development which had started in Italy extended over the whole of Europe, and it also meant that the period which Burckhardt described incorporated his ideas of what the modern world was. This notion was neither clear nor simple, but of great complexity. Burckhardt no longer had the optimistic confidence in the future he had felt in Berlin and Bonn, when he had believed that the future belonged to constitutional liberalism and that Germany would be the leader to a new and better world in Europe.[18] Burckhardt's view of the modern world and of its future now contained deeply critical, even pessimistic features. Thus his concern with the Italian Renaissance implied much more than a change of scholarly interests from northern to southern Europe. It encompassed the ambiguity of Burckhardt's view of the modern world, and this ambiguity was an essential factor in the impact that the book made and still makes. To grasp the notions about the role of culture, and therefore also about cultural history, expressed in *The Civilization of the Renaissance in Italy*, we must first understand the evolution of Burckhardt's views about the modern world.

Burckhardt's reflections and doubts about the modern age were first aroused in the 1840s while he was working in the field of art history. In revising Kugler's

---

[18] This is explained at greater length in my article mentioned in n. 1 above.

Handbook of the History of Painting he had followed Kugler's method and used what might be called an encyclopedic approach, presenting new periods of art as coinciding with new periods of history. On his travels to Italy, and, most of all, on his deeply satisfying and moving visits to the "unforgettable Rome," Burckhardt had begun to question this somewhat schematic procedure and even to become bored with it. He became convinced of the unique artistic achievements of the classical world and of the necessity of a qualitative approach in the consideration of works of art. He had undergone a conversion, as he explained in a letter to Paul Heyse: "For some time I have been making a full turn in my views of art. . . . I would never have believed that such an old, rotten cultural historian as myself, who imagined [himself] to be able to judge every point of view or epoch according to its own scale of values, could become so one-sided as I am. My eyes suddenly seemed to have opened, and I say to myself, as Saint Remigius said to Chlodwig: 'Incende quod adorasti, adora quod incendisti.' "[19] From that time on for Burckhardt really great art contained a classical element.

This "conversion" had its important consequences. It meant that Renaissance art gained special and unique importance for Burckhardt as an apex in art history. Burckhardt's earlier enthusiasm for Gothic art, which he had seen as man's greatest artistic achievement, waned. Moreover, there was no doubt in Burckhardt's mind that in the fifteenth and sixteenth centuries a new period of history—the modern age—had begun and that the art of the Renaissance was the

[19] Letter dated August 13, 1852, in *Briefe*, 3:161.

art of the modern age. Yet modern art had not remained on the level of its beginning in the Renaissance; it had, indeed, gone in very different directions,
and had never reached that level again. The relation of
art to the spirit of the age in which it arose and developed raised questions, therefore, that so far had never
been answered.

The importance of this question was intensified because Burckhardt's conversion to a new view about the
nature of great art was part of a broader, more fundamental change: Burckhardt distanced himself from
Germany. When, in 1843, after his student years in
Germany, he had returned to Switzerland, he had regarded Germany as the future leader of European culture and consequently had supported a closer connection between Switzerland and Germany. During the
three years that he spent in Basel lecturing at the university and editing Basel's leading conservative newspaper, his attitude toward politics changed. His views
became more conservative and rigidified. Burckhardt
had been shocked by the violence of political mass
demonstrations, and he became bitterly opposed to
"howling and shouting radicalism."[20] The mainte-
nance of the existing constitutional order was now
among his chief concerns.

When Burckhardt returned to Berlin in 1846, he expected that he would leave behind him the political
excesses that had disgusted him in Basel. He soon discovered that the political situation in Prussia was no
better, was in fact even worse than in Switzerland. In

---

[20] "Schweizerische Brüllradikalismus," in *Briefe*, 2:86, but similar expressions occur frequently. See also Burckhardt's newspaper
reports published in Emil Dürr, *Jacob Burckhardt als Politischer
Publizist* (Zurich, 1957), 43–161.

Prussia, too, he feared, radicalism would come forward and create dangers all over: "Nous dansons sur un volcan."[21] Burckhardt's fear of the turmoil that opposition to the government might bring about was deepened by the impact of the rising political unrest on his personal relations. Those who had been his friends when he studied in Berlin and Bonn, above all Gottfried Kinkel, belonged to the opposition and were raising radical demands and favoring political action. In a moving letter to Kinkel Burckhardt tells him that he cannot approve of his "political foolishnesses" but will continue to love him as a human being.[22] For Burckhardt, politics was dead. Burckhardt was in Rome when the revolution of 1848 broke out; it is characteristic that his sympathies lay on the side of the pope and that he had little tolerance for those who wanted to change the hierarchical government and bring about a closer union of all the Italian states.[23]

When Burckhardt arrived at this rejection of politics, a period of his life had come to its end. He was aware that for him the time of youth was over, and he abandoned all dreams of becoming a poet. Alteration in his views on art, rejection of politics and of liberal notions

[21] *Briefe*, 3:79; this letter to Andreas Heusler-Rybiner, dated July 9, 1847, gives a characteristic survey of Burckhardt's views on the political situation in Prussia. His entire correspondence of the years 1846–1849 reveals a steadily increasing distance from his former liberal views. In his letter of June 19, 1848, we find the revealing statement that he has become "discouraged with the nineteenth century." *Briefe*, 3:95.

[22] Letter dated December 6, 1846, in *Briefe*, 3:42–48.

[23] For remarks on the Roman situation, see *Briefe*, 3:96, but most of all, the very negative report about the Roman people in *Unbekannte Aufsätze Jakob Burckhardts aus Paris, Rom und Mailand*, ed. Josef Oswald (Basel, 1922), 135–149.

with which he once had sympathized, awareness that his literary ambitions had been a dream and a delusion—all these developments were interconnected. This thoroughgoing change manifested itself in his rejection of the North and his newfound admiration for the South.

Beyond aesthetic concerns and political experiences, however, this turn in Burckhardt's life was grounded in an inherited social attitude that placed a distance between him and the contemporary world. Burckhardt was repelled by the deep changes brought about by nineteenth-century industrialization. The masses emerging as a politically active force were for him only lower classes, not workers. The realism and the social concerns of novels and plays seemed to him mainly sensationalism, and he charged their authors with writing in pursuit of financial rewards.[24] Thus, behind Burckhardt's change in aesthetic taste and condemnation of political unrest lay a deeply rooted unwillingness to acknowledge the social changes tied to the economic developments of the nineteenth century. Going to Italy meant for him not only living in a better part of the world but living outside the contemporary world. And the wish to do so remained strong in him throughout his entire life.

Rejection of the course of modern culture involved a paradox that underlies Burckhardt's work on *The Civilization of the Renaissance in Italy.* He presents this period as a high point in the development of European culture, and at the same time as the root of a

[24] See Burckhardt's article, "Die französische Literatur und das Geld," written in Paris in 1843, published in *Unbekannte Aufsätze,* 60–68.

culture that became cheap, corrupt, and amoral. The solution of this contradiction lies in what Burckhardt considered to be the distinguishing attribute of the modern world: the discovery and widened use of man's capacities, in consequence of the discovery of the individual and individuality. The development of individuality opened the way to the great achievements of the Italian Renaissance in art and literature, because it provided a new vision of man's faculties and possibilities. However, this new vision also led to ruthless political actions and "unrestrained egoism in behavior." Side by side with profound corruption appeared artistic splendor and achievements of the noblest harmony. The Italian culture by itself was "neither good nor bad."[25]

In the Renaissance human capacities that until then had been restrained and suppressed were set free. Along with this emancipation, however, came centralization and urbanization, an increasing influence of the masses, and a popularization of taste and art— briefly, developments characteristic of the modern age; and they threatened to suffocate those human qualities on which originally the emergence of modern culture had been based.

Burckhardt never forgot that a scholar was also an educator. He did not believe in progress, nor did he view history as a steadily advancing process. He did not try to imagine what the future would be like; his criterion and measure was the past. The Renaissance was one of the great ages that enlightened us about the faculties of man and showed us what man's abilities could achieve, but the Renaissance also revealed the

[25] *Kultur der Renaissance*, in *Gesamtausgabe*, 5:329.

dangers inherent in the unrestricted use of man's capacities. The book was much more than a picture of the past. It was an analysis of the intellectual attitude and of the conditions from which modern culture had emerged, and it was also an appeal for awareness of the dangers that were involved in this development. Standing outside or above the contemporary world, Burckhardt felt he saw it from a distance, and that meant as a whole.

Because the notion of individuality is of constitutive importance to *The Civilization of the Renaissance in Italy*, the book presented a cultural history that, although following the chief requirements for a cultural history of its time, describing a particular epoch in all its aspects, at the same time deviated from this concept. *The Civilization of the Renaissance in Italy* is not concerned with the daily life of the period. The book gives no account of how people earned their living, how they dressed, how they kept peace and order in their towns. The chief concern of Burckhardt's book is the change brought about by the new awareness of man's individuality, by a new concept of man. The last two sections of the book, "Society and Festivals" and "Morality and Religion," show this very clearly. These were favorite topics of typical nineteenth-century cultural historians, who gave extended reports about the food offered at festivals, about the clothes people wore at home and at solemn occasions, and about religious rituals, baptisms, weddings, and processions. In Burckhardt's book, the section "Morality and Religion" has a different theme. It offers an analysis of the changes resulting from the weakening of the authority of the Church and from the development of a secular outlook: the appearance of superstition, of belief in magic and astrology, but also of an atheistic philosophy. The reader of this section will hardly be aware that the hold of the Church remained strong and that religious rituals continued to play an important role in life.

Likewise the section on "Society and Festivals" provides a significant illustration of what Burckhardt considered to be the decisive factor: it focuses exclusively on the development of new social attitudes. One topic discussed is the emergence of the idea of the "gentleman"; another highlights refinements in manners and in language, providing an analysis of the influence of literature and poetry on social behavior and conversation. It is characteristic that the treatment of these issues is not concerned with the people in general but with one section of society, its ruling group, whether that group consisted of the leading families of the city-republics or the members of the courts of the various princely states. Within these circles attention is focused on those who played an active part in the promotion of the new intellectual developments, mainly their promulgators, such as the humanists and poets, their sponsors and patrons, and individuals affected by these developments in their thought and behavior. Burckhardt states quite frankly that the Italian of the Renaissance, insofar as he was the "modern man," was an educated man. The Renaissance saw the emergence of an educated class, and for this reason it became the birthplace of the modern world. In Burckhardt's *Civilization of the Renaissance in Italy* cultural history has shifted from the description of the daily life of a period to an analysis of high culture.

IV.

In 1861/62, shortly after *The Civilization of the Renaissance in Italy* had appeared, Burckhardt envisaged a new project, a study of "the Greek spirit." Two years later he denied, however, that he had ever planned a book on this subject; what he had had in mind was a much less ambitious undertaking, a university course on Greek cultural history.[26] In October 1865, he withdrew from this project too: scholarly production in this field was so vast and so detailed that he did not feel in control of the material that was needed for such a course.[27]

These remarks are revealing. Burckhardt wavered between a book on the Greek spirit and a lecture course on Greek culture. Actually the four large volumes that were published in Burckhardt's collected works under the title *Greek Cultural History*[28] contain elements of both: they are a survey of Greek cultural achievements and an analysis of the Greek mind.

The project occupied Burckhardt throughout a decade. The plan is mentioned first in the early sixties, and ten years later, in January 1870, we hear that a lecture course on this subject had been worked out. This was not the only endeavor in which Burckhardt was engaged during the 1860s. Yet his other projects hardly interrupted or interfered with his concentration on Greek culture. For instance, Burckhardt published a book on Renaissance architecture that represented a continuation of the history of architecture of his friend, Franz Kugler, who had died in 1858. This volume was based on material that Burckhardt had assembled and prepared for publication more than ten years before, so this task absorbed relatively little of his time and energy.

[26] Letter to Otto Ribbeck, dated July 10, 1864, in *Briefe*, 4:155.
[27] *Briefe*, 4:197.
[28] The work, which is itself divided into four volumes, occupies vols. 8–11 of *Gesamtausgabe*.

In the winter of 1868/69, Burckhardt also offered for the first time a lecture series on the study of history;[29] but again, this undertaking did not divert him from his concern with the world of classical Greece. The problems of Greek culture were a primary focus of this course. Burckhardt's thesis in "The Study of History" is that the varieties in the life of nations and cultures are determined by differences in the weight given to the three factors which determine the formation of human society: state, religion, and culture. In Burckhardt's view, culture is different from the other two factors, state and religion. Whereas state and religion claim universal validity and feel justified to enforce their claim by coercion, the existence of culture depends on the possibility of individuals' moving freely in different directions, of spontaneity. None of these three forces exists by itself; they are always bound together, and the particular character of a culture is determined by the extent to which state and religion allow or restrict a free development. The Greek culture and the modern world exemplify that, at least for a time, culture can escape the embrace of state and religion and develop freely. In Burckhardt's view Athens certainly deserves the attention it has received—however, not because it was a political, but because it was a cultural center.[30]

[29] The course was then presented for the last time in the academic year 1872/73. It was published after Burckhardt's death in 1905 with the title *Weltgeschichtliche Betrachtungen* (Reflections on world history) and will be found in *Gesamtausgabe*, vol. 7. A much more authentic text, however, was published by Peter Ganz (Munich, 1982) with the more appropriate title *Über das Studium der Geschichte* (On the study of history), and this edition will be quoted in the following.

[30] Ibid., 318–319.

Thus the classical world was ever present in Burckhardt's lectures on the study of history, and the project
he had discussed in 1861/62 remained constantly in
his mind. In the course of the 1860s, the study of
Greek culture became even more interesting and more
urgent for Burckhardt. In October 1868, Burckhardt
wrote to a young nephew that in the preceding summer he had taught a course on Roman history, but that
he had felt oppressed by the immense amount of factual information which he had to pack in such a
course. He would never do that again; instead he was
now beginning to prepare a course on the Greek
spirit.[31] This sharp rejection of Rome in favor of
Greece is striking; the contribution of classical Greece
to the European intellectual world had gained new
weight in his mind.

Burckhardt's concern with the problem of Greek
culture was intensified and shaped by events on the
European political scene. With its victory in the war of
1866, Prussia had established itself as arbiter in Germany. This event seemed to have confirmed the views
of historians like Droysen and Mommsen—Burckhardt's *viri eruditissimi*—who regarded power as the
determining force in history and for whom history was
identical with political history. Burckhardt felt a
strong need to assert a different, an opposing point of
view. In Burckhardt's opinion the developments of the
following years, namely, the Franco-Prussian War,
placed European culture in still greater danger. Just before the outbreak of the war he expressed his uneasi-
ness about Prussia's dominating influence on German
life: "The great things that concentration can produce
are intellectually mediocre." If the German spirit by

---

[31] Letter to Jacob Oeri, October 24, 1868, in *Briefe*, 5:37.

its own inner strength does not fend off this domination by brutal force, he asserted, we are lost.[32] During
the Franco-Prussian War Burckhardt wrote that he had
no hope for a future in which there would be time and
a place for the arts and for the enjoyment of peace; "everyone will remain under arms." He was "deeply wor-
ried about the general fate of our culture." "We have
entered an era of wars in which many aspects we believed formed part of our intellectual life will be
thrown overboard as intellectual luxury."

This negative evaluation of the developments in the
modern world was the product of a long, gradual development. Burckhardt's outlook upon the contemporary scene had been troubled and discontented since
the late forties and the early fifties.[33] With the exception of his academic activity, he had endeavored to
withdraw from any involvement in the affairs of the
contemporary world. In the 1860s, this rejection of his
own time had taken a more pronounced, a more mag-
isterial and gloomy form. The name of Schopenhauer
begins to occur frequently in Burckhardt's correspondence. In a letter written on July 20, 1870—the day
after the French declaration of war against Prussia—
Schopenhauer appears to Burckhardt as the man who
had seen the inevitability of the coming doom: "Oh,
what revealing light radiates now from the philosopher."[34] The deepening and widening of Burckhardt's
pessimism had a decisive influence on his vision of

[32] Letter to Friedrich von Preen, July 3, 1870, in *Briefe*, 4:97; the
following remarks come from letters to Preen written on July 20,
September 27, December 31, 1870, and March 5, July 2, and October 12, 1871, all published in *Briefe*, 5.

[33] See above, p. 62.

[34] *Briefe*, 5:105, but Schopenhauer is also mentioned in letters to
Preen dated September 27, 1870, and December 31, 1870.

Greek culture and was a crucial element in the way he presented it.

The picture that emerged from Burckhardt's analysis of Greek culture emphasized that the Greeks were not happy people; life in Greece was harassed and dangerous. The idealized view of ancient Greece as a land of beauty and hope, which German neohumanism of the eighteenth century had created and which had found its transfiguration in Schiller's poem *The Gods of Greece*, was in Burckhardt's view "one of the greatest falsifications of historical judgments ever made."[35] Greek culture arose in a world ruled by arbitrary gods and in societies requiring obedience and full surrender of the individual. During only a very limited period of time, in the struggles against the powers of state and religion, was enough freedom attained to make cultural achievements possible. Certainly, in this contemptuous refusal to idealize Greek life, Burckhardt had predecessors and contemporaries among the scholars of his time. His teacher, Boeckh, had written in his famous work *The Athenian Economy* that the Greeks, "among the brilliance of art and the flourishing of freedom, were more unhappy than most people believe; they carried the seed of downfall in them." For the famous classicist Ernst Curtius, Greek culture flowered only during a short period, and Curtius painted a dark picture of the egoism, cruelty, and greed that Greek individualism had fostered. This fragility of Greek culture cast harsh light on the superficiality of modern culture because it raised doubts that the latter would

---

[35] *Gesamtausgabe*, 9:343; in general for Burckhardt's predecessors and his criticism of their views, see Kaegi's *Jacob Burckhardt*, 7:18–72.

have the strength to take up the struggle against those forces of politics and religion which stood in the way of freedom's development. With his picture of Greek culture, Burckhardt wanted to hold a mirror before the modern world. In this undertaking he was supported by a young colleague in Basel who also used the story of classical Greece as a means to criticize the values of the modern world. Burckhardt quotes Nietzsche's *Birth of Tragedy from the Spirit of Music* four times, approvingly, in his *Greek Cultural History*.[36] In the years when Burckhardt lectured on "The Study of History" and on Greek cultural history, Burckhardt and Nietzsche were in close intellectual contact.[37]

The combination of two different projects—a book on "the Greek spirit" and a lecture course at the university—gave Burckhardt's *Greek Cultural History* its richness and variety. These lectures contain a detailed and penetrating description of Sparta, usually the most unsympathetically treated Greek state. They make the arbitrary character of the Greek gods comprehensible as that of magnified human beings, but they also treat the belief in ghosts, demons, and prophesies as part of the Greek religion. They reveal the greatness of the *Iliad* and the *Odyssey* by emphasizing the coherence of their structure. An analysis of Greek tragedy culminates in a discussion of the works of Sophocles, in which, as Burckhardt explains, the events of life are determined by the interaction of fate and human psychology. Burckhardt's most memorable portrait of an

[36] *Griechische Kulturgeschichte*, 3:193, 223, 228; 4:385.

[37] The question of the relation between Burckhardt and Nietzsche has been so frequently discussed that I restrict myself to an analysis of the influence of these relations on the origin of Burckhardt's *Greek Cultural History*.

individual is that of Socrates, who possessed superiority of knowledge and, through devastating irony,
showed up everyone else's errors. Consequently, as
Burckhardt wrote, "everyone ran away whenever he
was seen coming around the corner." The most carefully worked out characterization is that of Thucydi-
des: "for all times the great pioneer" and "for us the
father of judging in terms of cultural history, that is,
in terms of the standards beneath which the world
ought never to sink."[38] Burckhardt's lectures in *Greek
Cultural History* treat topics of an almost confusing
diversity, and one must read this work very carefully
to become aware of its unifying theme.

In his lectures on "The Study of History" Burckhardt had said that culture is the embodiment of all
that serves the promotion of material life, but also that
it is an expression of spiritual and emotional life and
that it develops spontaneously. This formulation cor-
responded to what was then the predominant concept
of cultural history. But the lectures in *Greek Cultural
History* contain hardly any consideration of the conditions and forms of material life.[39] What had been
and, at the time of these lectures, still was considered
to be the chief content of cultural history—the description of daily life—is hardly touched upon.

The reason is that the lectures on Greek cultural
history were inspired by a different, deeply personal
concern. In Burckhardt's view, the study of Greek cul-

[38] *Griechische Kulturgeschichte*, 3:418.

[39] There is a discussion of slavery, but characteristically Burckhardt directs attention to the fact that almost all slaves were non-
Greeks and the existence of slavery therefore diminished the importance of economic and material factors, or even removed them
entirely from artistic and intellectual activities.

ture might help to elucidate the general problems of the rise and decline of culture; it might serve to clarify the relation of culture to politics and religion.

Burckhardt's picture of ancient Greece encompasses politics and religion, art and poetry, philosophy and scholarship. He emphasizes that the polis was in full control of the life and activities of its male inhabitants. The polis created equality of conditions, and under these circumstances superiority in competition (agon) was the only way a man might distinguish himself. An essential element of Greek culture, therefore, was its agonistic character. Competition also characterized the relations among the cities of Greece and Asia Minor, struggling with one another for domination. The agonistic character of Greek culture was further strengthened by religion; each polis had its own protecting gods or goddesses and its heroes. Their temples and festivities were an integral part of the life of the polis.

Individual freedom is a precondition for the creation of works of art and poetry, but in a situation of far-reaching, almost complete political control, the space for individual freedom could be gained only in hard struggles in which competitiveness and individualism were crucial factors. The freedom that was achieved in these struggles could maintain itself only for a brief moment. It was in Athens, in the time of Sophocles, that Greek culture reached its high point. The competitiveness that had helped to create freedom also destroyed it. The competition among numerous city-states was a weakness in relation to larger and more united non-Greek powers and resulted in the subjection of Greece to Macedonia and Rome. Burckhardt emphasizes the fragility of Greek culture. The entire last volume of the work depicts the slow and very gradual rise of Greek culture and its long decline in the Hellenistic period, underlining thereby the shortness of the period during which Greek culture had remained at its peak.

Burckhardt states that the life which existed in Greece "has never existed on earth either before or later or anywhere."[40] Nevertheless, the lectures are meant to be much more than the re-creation of a brilliant past; the book's underlying purpose is to confront modern culture with the culture of Greece. In Greece, competition among equals had brought all the capacities and forces of an individual into play and helped to develop them. The conditions that had made this development of human faculties possible no longer existed in the modern world. Economic activities had created inequalities and formed insuperable obstacles to the development of the powers of the individual. "Life has become pressing." A Greek was not driven by the need to make a living. His aim was "sudden, brilliant recognition," whereas the man of today chiefly works for a position that gives him security. Modern politics has created further obstacles to the development of culture, for the involvement in all aspects of social life that the small community demanded was no longer required in large modern states. Finally, the universalist claim of modern religion prevents the formation of close ties between social life and the veneration of god-protectors, a stimulus for art in Greece.

As Burckhardt's lectures on "The Study of History"

[40] *Gesamtausgabe*, 4:119; the following quotation comes from the same page.

show, state and religion were for him powers that in-
hibit the development of culture, and the analysis of
Greek culture showed the dangers which lay in the ex-
pansion of state and religion. That the modern world
appeared to be heading in the same direction seemed
to Burckhardt particularly tragic because the modern
world was not using the opportunities which it possessed—and which Greek culture had provided. Burckhardt's view of the Greeks is neither admiring, nor
even agreeable: they are rough and egoistic, lying and
unreliable, presumptuous and pessimistic; however,
they have brought to the world a gift that raises them
above all other peoples. They possessed and developed
the faculty to look upon the world objectively—as it
really was. Thus they widened the outlook of man beyond the small sphere in which he lived and enabled
him to extend his knowledge to other cultures. With
this gift of looking out beyond their own world, the
Greeks had been able to tie Europe and the Orient together and to lay the foundation of a world culture. By
making their culture an element of all further advances, they had assured the continuity of world history.

It was a long road that had led Burckhardt to this
view. In contrast to many, if not most of his contemporaries, he had not been captivated by the Hegelian
magic and had rejected all philosophical speculation
about the course of history. Not only was he, as he insisted, "no philosophical head"; he did not believe that
the course of history was determined by logic. Yet he
was a student of history and as such he could not
evade the question of what role a particular fact plays
in the general process of historical continuity. When
Burckhardt wrote the *Constantine* he realized that the

detailed description of human activities which the cultural historian was then expected to provide was incompatible with what had been the crucial development of this period: the Christianization of the Roman Empire. Although cultural history might add to the picture of a past period, it did not contribute to the pursuit of history's central concern, the explanation and understanding of the advances of world history. In his *Civilization of the Renaissance in Italy* Burckhardt did not have to face this issue because the very subject of his book was a world-historical event: the birth of modern man. In the *Greek Cultural History* the central importance of continuity in world history emerges as his chief concern; he considered it as dependent on man's acting as guardian and continuator of the intellectual traditions of the past. Thus history was to keep humanity aware of those intellectual traditions, a task very different from the one he set himself when, thirty years before, he had decided to become a cultural historian.

CHAPTER V

BURCKHARDT AND THE CULTURAL
HISTORY OF HIS TIME

THE LECTURE COURSE on Greek cultural history
that Burckhardt gave at Basel in 1872 opened
with an introduction explaining the aims and
method of the course.[1] Only in these pages did Burckhardt discuss theoretical aspects of his work in cultural history.

The introduction contains what we might expect,
beginning with an explanation of how this course differs from other courses on Greek culture. Burckhardt
explains that his course will not deal with what is
done in courses on Greek antiquities, that is, it will
not discuss in detail the structure and organizations of
Greek public and private life, nor will it duplicate
courses on Greek history: it will not be a factual
chronological account. Instead the course will encour-
age the student to read literary sources, preferably in

[1] Burckhardt's *Griechische Kulturgeschichte* represents vols. 8–
11 of the *Gesamtausgabe* (Stuttgart, 1930–1933) of his works. The
introduction ("Einleitung"), with which this essay is chiefly concerned, will be found in 8:1–11. In Werner Kaegi's Burckhardt biography—*Jacob Burckhardt Eine Biographie* (Basel, 1947–1982)—
the *Griechische Kulturgeschichte* is discussed in vol. 7, and there,
opposite 82, appear reproductions of two manuscript pages of the
introduction. At the head of the first of these we find the date May
6, 1872. Kaegi has not dealt with the introduction at any length.

the original, thus contributing to the enjoyment that comes from acquaintance with Greek literature, and, still more importantly, creating an awareness of permanent intellectual values.

Between the explanation of the particular character of this course on Greek cultural history and the description of its pedagogical purpose, Burckhardt inserted a middle section in his introduction in which he outlined his methodology. There the focal point is his concept of cultural history.

At the time when Burckhardt wrote the introduction, the question of the value of cultural history and of its relation to political history was a much-debated issue. In order to understand Burckhardt's view of cultural history as expressed in this introduction, we must consider the state of this debate.[2] In the earlier part of the nineteenth century there was no real con-

---

[2] In twentieth-century treatments of the development of German historiography, the development of cultural history is remarkably neglected. Ernst Schaumkell, *Geschichte der deutschen Kulturgeschichtschreibung* (Leipzig, 1905), has only a vague notion of cultural history and his book is not very helpful. Georg von Below, *Die deutsche Geschichtschreibung von den Befreiungskriegen bis zu unsern Tagen* (Munich, 1924), states the main facts, although his cannot be regarded as a very objective analysis. Among works written in the nineteenth century and in the early stages of the Lamprecht-Streit, see the books by Wesendonck and Jodl mentioned below in nn. 9 and 10; a brief illuminating survey will be found in the introductory section of Henry Simonsfeld, *Wilhelm Heinrich Riehl als Kulturhistoriker* (Munich, 1898), with extensive bibliography. Developments in the first half of the nineteenth century are hardly touched upon in these writings. I have discussed them briefly in my article, "Jacob Burckhardt's Student Years: The Road to Cultural History," *Journal of the History of Ideas* 47 (1986): 249–274, and see also, for the period before the middle of the nineteenth century, the preceding chapter.

trast or rivalry between political and cultural history: cultural history existed as a recognized field of scholarship and was regarded as complementary rather than separate from or antithetical to political history. Cultural history was pursued along two different lines. One approach had its origin in the Enlightenment idea of human progress, and the goal was to define and explain the various stages of this process. The other approach was very much like what is now called social history: description of the forms and activities of life in past centuries. In the second half of the nineteenth century the work of the cultural historian became more precise. With the appearance of Darwin's *Origin of Species* the evolution of culture became tied to the notion of the fight for existence; works that used Darwin's theories to explain the course of world history, like Friedrich von Hellwald's *Cultural History in Its Natural Development*,[3] were widely read. The other approach to cultural history—the study of the social life of the past—was increasingly influenced by Romanticism and nationalism. The study of attitudes and the conditions of life was seen as having the purpose of recognizing and defining the particular character of a nation or of the peoples of a region or area. In the fifties of the nineteenth century this approach was represented by two widely known and extremely popular writers: by the scholarly studies on urban and rural society by W. H. Riehl and the more journalistic "pictures from the German past" by Gustav Freytag.[4]

[3] Friedrich von Hellwald, *Kulturgeschichte in ihrer natürlichen Entwicklung bis zur Gegenwart* (Augsburg, 1875); Burckhardt refers several times to Hellwald in his *Greek Cultural History*, mostly disapprovingly.

[4] Both Riehl and Freytag have been discussed in their importance

In 1852, the Germanic Museum was founded in Nuremberg for the purpose of promoting patriotic feeling through knowledge of the past.[5] Johannes Falke and Johann Müller, who had been active in establishing the Germanic Museum, in 1856 became editors of a journal exclusively devoted to cultural history. Characteristic of the connection between romantic nationalism and cultural history was its title *Journal for German Cultural History;* it bore the subtitle *Views and Features of the Life of the German People.*[6] Its first volume contained essays on marriage proceedings in the fifteenth century and witch trials, fashions in hairdressing in the sixteenth century and vice squads in the seventeenth, descriptions of dances and analysis of anti-Jewish satires, information about military and trade routes and instruction in archery.[7] It would seem

---

for the history of historiography in the well-known handbook by Eduard Fueter, *Geschichte der Neueren Historiographie* (Munich, 1925); Simonsfeld, *Wilhelm Heinrich Riehl,* is of interest as a contemporary evaluation. Freytag's *Bilder aus der deutschen Vergangenheit* began to appear in 1859 and were continued through the 1860s.

[5] A detailed history of the Germanic Museum is *Das Germanische Nationalmuseum Nürnberg 1852–1977: Beiträge zu einer Geschichte,* ed. B. Deneke and R. Kahsnitz (Nuremberg, 1978); but see also the article "Germanisches Museum" in *Brockhaus Konversationslexikon* of 1865.

[6] The original title was *Zeitschrift für deutsche Kulturgeschichte—Bilder und Züge aus dem Leben des deutschen Volkes;* in 1891, there appeared a "Neue Folge" with the title "Zeitschrift für deutsche Kulturgeschichte." In 1894 the title became *Zeitschrift für Kulturgeschichte,* and in 1903 *Archiv für Kulturgeschichte.* It continues under this title.

[7] See the table of contents of the first volume of 1856, but the subjects of the articles in later volumes are not very different.

that there was hardly an aspect of social life from the fifteenth to the eighteenth century that was not covered in the articles of this journal of cultural history.

Undoubtedly political events contributed to this increased interest in the way people had lived in the various regions of Germany. The revolution of 1848 had been an attempt to overcome the fragmentation of Germany and to establish a centralized government. Those who had opposed this movement were anxious to show that the autonomy of the German states had roots in the way people lived in these various regions.[8] Moreover, it was probably more satisfactory to ascribe the failure of the revolution to conditions grounded in the past than to weakness and political errors. Thus cultural history in Germany assumed a conservative aspect. However, the revival of liberalism in the late fifties—and, still more, the demonstration of the crucial importance of political power by Bismarck's policy in the sixties, which led to the unification of the Reich—made the issues of political organization and power focal points of historical study. The dominant position that was now given to political history was well expressed by Wesendonck in his book on German historiography, which appeared a few years after the foundation of the Reich: "Even if we admit that the exclusive concentration on political history as we find it in the writings of many modern historians is too one-sided, we must acknowledge that political history

[8] See the characterization of the "bürgerlich-volkstümliche Geschichtsbewegung des 19. Jahrhunderts" in the article by Jürgen Kocka, "Geschichte als Aufklärung?" in *Die Zukunft der Aufklärung*, ed. J. Rüsen, E. Lämmert, and P. Glotz (Frankfurt am Main, 1988), 91–98.

must always be the foundation of historical work."[9] Nevertheless, the debate between political and cultural history continued, although cultural history was now forced back into a defensive position. Its advocates maintained that cultural history had its own particular issues, such as the struggle of man with nature and the gradual mastery of natural forces through work and technology.[10] They insisted that the study of cultural history was not pursued in a dilettante manner[11] but according to strict scholarly principles— that cultural history had its own method: it did not look for the particular and individual but for what was typical.[12] The claims for cultural history were now

[9] H. Wesendonck, *Die Begründung der neueren deutschen Geschichtsschreibung durch Gatterer und Schlözer nebst Einleitung über Gang und Stand derselben vor diesen* (Leipzig, 1876), 129: "Aber wenn wir auch zugeben, dass die fast ausschliessliche Pflege der politischen Geschichte, wie sie jetzt auf Kosten der Culturgeschichte von sehr vielen modernen Geschichtsschreibern ausgeübt wird, viel zu einseitig ist, so müssen wir doch auch gestehen, dass die politische Geschichte stets die Grundlage für den Historiker bilden muss." English quotations in this chapter are usually my translations from German writings not previously translated into English, but I give the original German text in footnotes to avoid misunderstandings.

[10] See, for instance, Friedrich Jodl, *Kulturgeschichtsschreibung, ihre Entwicklung und ihr Problem* (Halle, 1878); on 112, Jodl lists as the concerns of cultural history (1) the struggle of man with nature, (2) the striving of man toward coexistence through the formation of associations, and (3) the aspiration toward an ideal.

[11] The *Zeitschrift für deutsche Kulturgeschichte* 1 (1856) contains an article, "Der Dilettantismus in der Kulturgeschichte," that is especially concerned with the rejection of dilettantism. See also in the same issue the article by Johannes Falke, "Die Deutsche Kulturgeschichte," particularly 20ff.

[12] See Georg Steinhausen's article, "Professoren der Kulturge-

somewhat reduced but at the same time more firmly grounded by the assertion that cultural history had a particular, clearly defined field of research. Consequently the demand was raised for the establishment of special chairs of cultural history;[13] briefly, a retreat into specialization took place. Nevertheless, the comparative value of political and cultural history for an understanding of the past remained a burning issue. It was vehemently debated between two well-known German historians, Eberhard Gothein and Dietrich Schäfer.[14]

Gothein explained that cultural history placed before our eyes the entire development of human thought and human attitudes; cultural history could demand, therefore, the subordination of political history to this comprehensive goal. Gothein pointed to Burckhardt's *Civilization of the Renaissance* as a model of work in cultural history.

Dietrich Schäfer admitted that Jacob Burckhardt had "a subtle political mind," that he was a "true historian," who had written a "brilliant book." But he emphasized that the first part of the *Civilization of the Renaissance* was concerned with political history and showed that the issues raised by cultural history could

---

schichte?" in *Zeitschrift für Kulturgeschichte* 2 (1895): 195: "Es kommt darauf an, in der Masse der Einzelheiten das Typische zu erkennen und festzustellen." See also Jodl, *Kulturgeschichtsschreibung*, 115ff. and similar remarks at many other places.

[13] See the article by Steinhausen mentioned in the preceding note; it contains references to literature on the same subject.

[14] The relevant writings are Eberhard Gothein, *Die Aufgaben der Kulturgeschichte* (Leipzig, 1889), and Deitrich Schäfer, *Geschichte und Kulturgeschichte; Eine Erwiderung* (Jena, 1891).

be answered only "when political life is established as the center of historical research." This discussion between Gothein and Schäfer has its special interest as the final event in the nineteenth-century debate about the value of political and cultural history. From the early 1890s on, Karl Lamprecht's *German History* began to appear, and in it he explained politics in psychological and cultural terms, arousing such a vehement rejection by the majority of influential German historians that in the following decades cultural history remained almost exorcised from the German academic world. Political history triumphed; it was the only accepted and recognized approach.[15]

Burckhardt had begun to lecture on Greek cultural history and to write his introduction to this course in 1872, after the German victory in the war against France. At that time, the debate between political and cultural history was still underway, although the pendulum was beginning to swing in the direction of political history. Burckhardt's introduction is clearly related to this literary struggle. Burckhardt wanted to mark out his own position in this debate on the relation between political and cultural history. He emphasizes strongly that he is an advocate of cultural history: cultural history, he states, is equal to political history. Cultural history possesses full scholarly reliability. The source materials on which cultural histories are built are even more authentic than those of po-

---

[15] There remained a few well-known historians—like Lamprecht or Kurt Breysig—who considered themselves cultural historians. For the outsider position of these historians, the article by Bernhard vom Brocke, "Kurt Breysig," in *Deutsche Historiker*, ed. H. U. Wehler (Göttingen, 1972), 5:95–116, is of interest.

litical history.[16] In political history a careful and extended examination is required to establish the correctness of a fact, and even then the results frequently remain doubtful. The sources of cultural history, however, have "primum gradum certitudinis." The cultural historian does not want to learn from his sources the "facts" of the past; he studies the sources because they express the spirit of former times. It does not matter, therefore, whether they are factually correct, whether they lie or indulge in exaggerations or inventions. Even misleading statements may tell us something about the mind of a former age. In summing up the central notions that ought to inform the interest of a cultural historian, Burckhardt writes: "History is concerned with the inner life of past humanity and states what people were, what they wanted, thought, were able to see and able to do. . . . What was wanted and what was assumed is as important as what actually happened; what people saw was as important as what they did."[17]

Although the establishment of a factual foundation is not the center of the cultural historian's work, cultural history does not lack in method. The cultural historian has to be as strict in the application of methodical principles as the political historian. For the cultural historian the decisive criterion in the evaluation of his sources must be whether certain attitudes and expressions can be found in great frequency and serve as a means of communication over a long period.

[16] For the following, see most of all "Einleitung," 3.

[17] "Sie geht auf das Innere der vergangenen Menschheit und verkündet, was diese war, wollte, dachte, schaute und vermochte. . . . Das Gewollte und Vorausgesetzte also ist so wichtig als das Geschehene, die Anschauung so wichtig als irgendein Tun."

Briefly, the primary interest of a cultural historian must be whether what his sources say is typical and constant.[18]

Burckhardt is aware that what he outlines as characteristic of cultural history is very much his own opinion. However, because all these questions are under dispute, because "all historical communication at the universities is in a crisis," he concludes that "we can move most freely,"[19] that he has the right to follow his own course. He considers himself to be a cultural historian and defends cultural history; he has the right to follow his own path.

In his early years, Burckhardt regarded the study and description of the external conditions of life as the main task of cultural history, and this was still seen as a primary task of cultural history when Burckhardt wrote his introduction in the early 1870s. But to Burckhardt this now appeared a task of inferior importance.[20] He also rejected another task assigned to cultural history—the study of man's ascent to higher forms of existence; he did not believe that humanity had improved in the course of history. His low opinion of the culture of his own time is well reflected in the

[18] See "Einleitung," 3–4: "Aber auch wenn eine berichtete Tat in Wahrheit garnicht oder doch nicht so geschehen ist, so behält die Anschauung, die sie als geschehen oder in einer bestimmten Form geschehen voraussetzt ihren Wert durch das Typische der Darstellung . . . vielleicht ist aber das Konstante, das aus diesen typischen Darstellungen hervorgeht, der wahrste 'Realinhalt' des Altertums."

[19] "Ohnehin liegt alle historische Mitteilung an den Universitäten in einer Krisis, welche jeden nötigen kann, eigene Wege einzuschlagen. . . . So können wir uns sehr frei bewegen" (3).

[20] "Auch verzichten wir auf die Behandlung dessen, was nur dem gewöhnlichen äussern Leben angehört." For this and the following see "Einleitung," 6 and 7.

statement that those who "have become slaves of present-day literature which speaks primarily to our nerves" and who "depend on newspaper reading" will never be able to understand the Greek world.[21]

Neither the widening of knowledge of external conditions nor acquisition of insight into the stages of world historical development appeared to Burckhardt to be worth the effort. We must ask, then, what remained as the purpose of cultural history in his view.

In Burckhardt's view the foremost and most fundamental requirement in the study of cultural history was the intense and careful reading of the literary works of the past.[22] Through such reading the student of cultural history would come into direct contact with the working of a creative mind; he would gain a feeling for values and standards; he would become aware of what is transitory and what is of lasting value. Behind the development and changes that seem to dominate the life of the past and the present, he would be able to discern what remains unchanged. He would become aware of the true, enduring values in a world absorbed in the momentary. Cultural history would reveal what are, or should be, permanent standards.

Burckhardt was born in the age of neohumanism; by confronting the modern world with the cultural

[21] "Freilich muss man nicht bereits völlig der jetzigen Literatur (die soviel unmittelbarer zu unsern Nerven spricht) verfallen sein. Und vollends nicht dem Zeitungslesen."

[22] "Alles, was dem Tage angehört, geht leicht und vorzugsweise eine Verbindung ein mit dem Materiellen in uns, mit unsern Interessen; das Vergangene *kann* wenigstens eher sich verbinden mit dem Geistigen in uns, mit unserm höhern Interesse." See "Einleitung," 7–10.

achievements of Greece, he expressed a view that had been present in his mind since his early years. Why and how the classical era ended had been the theme of his *Constantine.* In *The Civilization of the Renaissance* the ancient world had been the stimulus that led to the birth of modern man. When his main concern had turned to the upholding of true values in a world that he thought was in decline, he again returned to Greece to show what man's true accomplishments were. "Eternally we shall remain the admirers of the Greeks for what they achieved and were able to achieve, and eternally we shall remain in their debt for their insight into the world."[23]

We may not share Burckhardt's pessimistic outlook about the world in which we live, but it is his greatness that in his writings—more than in those of any other historian—the study of the past forces us to examine what we are.

[23] "Und so werden wir ewig im Schaffen und Können die Bewunderer und in der Weltkenntnis die Schuldner der Griechen bleiben. Hier sind sie uns nahe, dort gross, fremd und ferne. Und wenn die Kulturgeschichte dies Verhältnis klarer hervorhebt, als die Geschichte der Ereignisse, so darf sie für uns den Vorzug vor dieser haben" (11).

CHAPTER VI

'''''||||||||''''

RANKE AND BURCKHARDT: THE

COMMON BOND

R ANKE AND BURCKHARDT are the two greatest historical thinkers whom the nineteenth century has produced within the area of German culture. With these words the eighty-six-year-old Friedrich Meinecke began in 1948 his address "Ranke and Burckhardt."[1] This is only one, although one of the most distinguished, of the many contributions to a much-discussed subject. Frequently, one might almost say usually, this theme is treated as a confrontation. Ranke believed in the power of the state as guardian of order and stability; Burckhardt regarded power as tied to evil. Ranke, the Protestant scholar, confidently sought the hand of a benevolent God in the events of the past; Burckhardt, skeptical and withdrawn, saw in history an unending struggle among antagonistic forces. The central issue in all the reflections on Ranke and Burckhardt is the difference between a political and a cultural approach to history: between political and cultural history.

In this concluding chapter a different, almost contrary issue will be discussed. Its subject will be the

[1] Friedrich Meinecke, *Werke*, vol. 7, *Zur Geschichte der Geschichtsschreibung* (Munich, 1968), 93: "Ranke und Burckhardt sind die beiden grössten historischen Denker, die das 19. Jahrhundert innerhalb der deutschen Kulturnation hervorgebracht hat."

bonds that tied Ranke and Burckhardt together, and the attempt will be made to explain why, despite differences in historical interest and approach, they respected and appreciated each other's achievements.[2] That Ranke assigned great importance to Burckhardt's works is suggested by his repeated recommendation of Burckhardt to the newly established chair of history at the University of Munich in 1852; it was an appointment in which Ranke, because of his friendship with the Bavarian king, took the greatest interest. Burckhardt expressed his admiration for Ranke's work on two occasions, and these two statements give insight into what constituted a common bond between the two.[3] The first of these statements is in the curriculum vitae that accompanied the submission of Burckhardt's dissertation to the Faculty of the University of Basel in 1843; the other may be found in the retrospect of his life that he composed in 1889 to be read, in accordance with the customs of Basel, at his funeral.

It is only appropriate that a curriculum vitae written for an academic body should name the teachers under whom the applicant studied. Burckhardt's mention of Ranke on the list of his teachers stands out because of its length. Burckhardt says that he had been particularly fortunate in his historical studies because he had had as a teacher "a man who could not be praised enough, Leopold Ranke, who, not only through his teaching but also through his ever-ready advice, was willing to further me."[4]

---

[2] Werner Kaegi, *Jacob Burckhardt Eine Biographie* (Basel, 1947–1982), 2:72–73.

[3] The two statements can be found in ibid., 72.

[4] "Sed plurimum mihi gratulor, quod in historia magistrum nactus sum virum omni laude maiorem Leopoldum Ranke, qui non

Burckhardt had reason to emphasize that he was a disciple of Ranke; Ranke was then becoming recognized as the leading historian in the German-speaking world. When Burckhardt abandoned theology and decided to study history, his reason for going to Berlin was Ranke's presence there.[5] And from his second semester on, as long as he was in Berlin, Burckhardt never failed to attend Ranke's lectures and seminars.[6] The two men differed sharply in their outlook upon the social world. The young Basel patrician—moving, in his student years, chiefly in liberal circles—was contemptuous of Ranke's concern with rank and position. Burckhardt's disapproval of Ranke's civil-service attitude did not extend, however, to the work of the scholar. In a letter from Berlin Burckhardt wrote that "Ranke has never spoken about history in a frivolous manner. . . . The seriousness of history penetrates in a distinct, almost uncanny manner his deeply furrowed features."[7] Burckhardt himself stated soon after he had begun to attend Ranke's seminar that he now had an inkling of what history really was.[8] Here he probably alludes first of all to Ranke's critical method: the pre-

---

solum scholis suis, sed etiam praestantissimo consilio studia mea iuvare dignatus est."

[5] For a detailed discussion of Burckhardt's studies in Berlin, see my article "Jacob Burckhardt's Student Years: The Road to Cultural History," *Journal of the History of Ideas* 47 (1986): 249–274.

[6] See Otto Markwart, *Jacob Burckhardt Persönlichkeit und Jugendjahre* (Basel, 1920), 397–398.

[7] Jacob Burckhardt, *Briefe* (Basel, 1949), 1:160: "Nie hat man aus Ranke's Munde die geringste Frivolität gehört . . . wenn er von grossen Momenten spricht, so lagert sich der historische Ernst deutlich, ja halb unheimlich in seine tiefgefurchten Züge."

[8] Ibid., 157–158.

eminent importance of contemporary sources for the reconstruction of "wie es eigentlich gewesen." The influence of Ranke's teaching on Burckhardt, however, went much further than this. Burckhardt's first two lengthier historical studies—his *Carl Martell* and his *Konrad von Hochstaden*[9]—both written for Ranke's seminar, fitted in method and form the series called *Jahrbücher des Deutschen Reiches*, which Ranke had initiated and whose individual volumes were the work of the chief members of Ranke's seminar. In these two studies Burckhardt placed full emphasis on the concepts that Ranke regarded as the principal constituent elements of medieval Europe: the conquest of the Germanic world by Christianity, a society of Germanic-Romance nations, and Christianity as the uniting bond. In the studies on Swiss history that Burckhardt undertook after his return to Basel, he again followed Ranke's path, investigating in detail events of the Swiss Counter-Reformation on which Ranke had touched in his *History of the Popes*.[10] Burckhardt's dependence on his teacher shows itself most clearly in the lectures on the history of the Middle Ages that he gave in Basel in 1844/45—the first course he offered as a university teacher.[11] Probably Burckhardt saw a greater break between the Middle Ages and the modern world than Ranke did, but a comparison of the

[9] Both printed in *Jacob Burckhardt Gesamtausgabe*, vol. 1, *Frühe Schriften* (Stuttgart, 1930).

[10] See Burckhardt's articles in *Archiv für Schweizerische Geschichte* 6 (1849), 7 (1851), 8 (1851).

[11] The following is based on the notes that Burckhardt took in Berlin, where he heard Ranke's course on the "History of the Middle Ages," and on Burckhardt's notes for his own course in Basel.

THE COMMON BOND   « 97

notes that Burckhardt took in Ranke's course with his notes for his own course shows that in organization and factual information—from the emphasis placed on the importance of the struggle between Western and Eastern Europe to the books listed in the bibliography—Burckhardt's lectures were closely based on those of Ranke. Thus, when Burckhardt began his academic career he was a historian of the Ranke school, and the gratitude that he expressed in his curriculum vitae is a truthful reflection of the relation which at that time existed between Ranke and Burckhardt.

It is remarkable and somewhat surprising, however, that more than forty years later, in writing his own obituary, Burckhardt again found it important to emphasize that he had been a student of Ranke's. He wrote there that he had had the good fortune to present in Ranke's seminar two lengthy historical studies and to be rewarded by the praise of the great teacher.[12]

Prior to writing these remarks, Burckhardt had frequently expressed his dislike of the *viri eruditissimi* who dominated historical scholarship in Germany, many of whom had been Ranke's disciples. Furthermore Burckhardt believed that historical scholarship was going astray by concentrating on national histories and fostering nationalism and national conflicts.[13]

[12] "Er hatte das Glück, für Rankes Seminar zwei umfangreiche Arbeiten zu liefern und die Zufriedenheit des grossen Lehrers zu empfangen."

[13] In this respect it is quite interesting that, when Ranke's works were published in the seventies, the edition started with his so-called national histories; his *History of the Popes*, the earliest of the great works which had founded his fame, appeared as late as vol. 38.

And finally, political and cultural history were emerging as distinct, even incompatible approaches to the past, and Ranke was the recognized head of the school of political history, while Burckhardt had written the most outstanding work of cultural history.

Why then did Ranke remain for Burckhardt a determining element in his historical thinking? This is a question of significance because it focuses our attention on aspects of Ranke's historical thought that are overlooked when he is chiefly seen as Germany's leading political historian. A letter of Burckhardt's from his later years suggests an explanation. Burckhardt wrote to his friend Friedrich von Preen that he envied Preen because the latter was only now, in his mature years, beginning to read Ranke.[14] He, Burckhardt, considered *The History of the Popes* and the first volume of *German History in the Age of the Reformation* to be Ranke's real masterworks. He had read them as a student, and he had known passages of them by heart. He felt that in the *French History* something was lacking, and he found the *English History* somewhat boring; in the French and English histories the perspective and the criteria of universal history were wanting.[15]

We are now inclined to regard Ranke's oeuvre as a great unit, each of its parts expressing the same message about the principles and methods that ought to guide historical scholarship. The distinctions that Burckhardt draws among Ranke's histories, his emphasis on differences, even of a qualitative nature, among them, might warn us against accepting such a view of the uniform character of Ranke's works.

[14] *Briefe* (Basel, 1963), 5:263.
[15] "weil ihm hier der universalhistorische Athem und Masstab ausgeht."

Only Ranke's first two extended histories, *The History of the Popes* and *German History in the Age of the Reformation*, had Burckhardt's full approval and admiration. *The History of the Popes* had been published a few years before Burckhardt came as a student to Berlin. Ranke's work on the Reformation began to appear while he was studying there. Undoubtedly Burckhardt's view of these works reflects something of the impression that they made when they were first published. It is significant that Burckhardt remembered having known passages from them by heart. Clearly these histories were evaluated and appreciated as works of literary art. Indeed, we are still greatly impressed by Ranke's literary power when, for instance, we read Ranke's report about Luther's entry on a covered wagon into Leipzig for the disputation with Eck— it seems like a sixteenth-century woodcut come to life[16]—or when we read Ranke's description of the aging Charles V walking, protected from the heat of the sun by the foliage of closely planted chestnut trees, from the monastery of Saint Juste to his favorite hermitage.[17] Admittedly, in Germany and in France (one might think of Schiller and Johannes von Müller, or, in Ranke's time, of Thierry and Michelet) history had been treated by great writers. But the conjunction of literary art with accurate scholarship was a unique feature of Ranke's first two great histories. Before this time when histories had been the result of archival research, Burckhardt wrote, the past had been presented "in labyrinthine paragraphs," and history had declined in popularity because of the boring manner in which the historians had strung together one fact after the

[16] Ranke, *Sämmtliche Werke* (Leipzig, 1868–1890), 1:280.
[17] Ibid., 5:304 (in the section called "Last Days of Charles V").

other. Under the impression of his studies with Ranke Burckhardt wrote: "I have made a vow. Through my entire life I shall write a legible style."[18]

There was another feature in these two works that must have made them particularly attractive for Burckhardt. Nobody who knows Ranke's histories can say that they are exclusively concerned with political history. Every one of his great histories contains a chapter called "Outlook on the Literature." In the *English History*, however, Ranke writes: "It is not the times of great political struggles that are most favorable for literary and artistic production, but rather those times which precede them or follow them."[19] Thus, in the *English History*, which centers on the English Civil War, he rapidly surveys the literature of the preceding Elizabethan age from Bacon to Shakespeare. And in the *French History*, which has as its main theme the French religious wars of the sixteenth century, he describes the intellectual outlook of Descartes, Corneille, and Pascal within the framework of an outline of the Age of Louis XIV. These discussions of art and literature belong to the introductory and the concluding sections of the English and French histories, and in that sense they are not part of the great conflicts which form the center of these works. This cannot be said, however, about the treatment of aspects of cultural history in *The History of the Popes* and in *German History in the Age of the Reformation*. In these works the treatment of literature is not only more detailed, but the titles of the relevant sections—

[18] These are quotations from a letter to Gottfried Kinkel, March 21, 1842, in *Briefe* (Basel, 1949), 1:197.

[19] *Sämmtliche Werke*, 15:87.

"Changes in the Intellectual Direction," "Tendencies of Popular Literature," "Development of Literature"— indicate that they are integrated into the overarching story and treated either as reflecting the political developments or as influencing their course. To Burckhardt, for whom these two histories formed the introduction to Ranke's oeuvre, political and cultural history cannot have appeared to be sharply separated. What must have particularly impressed and delighted the young Burckhardt, who was also studying art history, was that, in *The History of the Popes*, the chapter on intellectual developments not only contained a long analysis of Ariosto and Tasso but also—and this cannot be found in any of Ranke's other works—a detailed discussion of painting and painters, from the Caracci to Domenichino and Guercino.[20]

Burckhardt, however, admired Ranke not only because the latter was a great writer whose histories embraced art and literature. There is a more fundamental consensus between Ranke's attitude in his early masterworks and Burckhardt's approach to history. In his letter to Preen Burckhardt praised as a distinguishing feature of Ranke's early volumes that he looks upon the past from the point of view of universal history. It is the fading of this perspective that, in Burckhardt's view, makes Ranke's later histories inferior to the two great works of his early years. There is a famous but also somewhat startling sentence in the preface to Ranke's *English History* that suggests a change of approach from Ranke's earlier to his later works and might indicate what Burckhardt had in mind. Ranke

[20] In the chapter on "Changes in the Intellectual Direction" in the fourth book of *The History of the Popes*.

wishes to justify his writing about the history of a nation to which he does not belong by birth. He explains that when an author undertakes such a task, he should not try to compose that country's national history but should deal only with those epochs when the history of the nation had strong influence on the course of events in other parts of Europe. These sentences reflect something of the intellectual climate of the second half of the nineteenth century, with its increasing emphasis on national history—an emphasis Burckhardt disliked—and it seems an approach very different and distant from the one that patterned Ranke's earlier works. Then Ranke wrote about developments that had a common European origin and patterned the entire development of European history; Ranke concerned himself with German history because it was in Germany that the new movement of the Reformation first emerged. European history was seen as a great stream into which many currents flowed and the entry of a new current was a historical subject of supreme importance. We must realize that the same notion shaped Burckhardt's outlook on the past. He wrote not a *Civilization of the Italian Renaissance* but a *Civilization of the Renaissance in Italy*, for among the peoples of Europe the Italian was the first modern man.

Yet the idea of universal history (which in the case of Ranke and Burckhardt is identical with European history) encompasses a problem that is fundamental and decisive for an understanding of the relationship between Ranke and Burckhardt, a problem that shows most clearly what divides them and what binds them together. This is the problem of historical continuity. Although an ever-present issue in history, it had come to the fore in its full importance and complexity in the

French Revolution. In the years when Ranke wrote his first two masterworks and Burckhardt studied under him, the stability established after Napoleon's fall had again been shaken. "We are dominated by a feeling of the provisional, of being frail and being threatened. Our time is characterized by uncertainty about the future," stated Burckhardt at the beginning of his lecture on the history of the French Revolution.[21] He said he would try to show how the present had developed from the past.[22] This became the central issue that gave value to the search for an understanding of the past and stimulated the development of modern historical scholarship. Certainly, the answers that Ranke and Burckhardt gave were widely different. Burckhardt, averse to the descent into mass rule and vulgarization, was convinced that, in the meaningless struggle of different and contrary human needs, what alone was worth preserving was the heritage of culture and of conditions of life which would allow human creativity. "We can try to preserve for better ages the fruits of the old time."[23] Ranke felt sure that, "as violent as the Revolution had been, it did not break off the preceding development of nations from the European culture."[24]

[21] "Das Glücksgefühl, das uns beherrscht, ist das Gefühl des Provisorischen, Hinfälligen und Bedrohten. Unsere Zeit charakterisiert die Unsicherheit der Zukunft."

[22] "Unser gegenwartiges Rechtsgefühl beruht darauf: die Gleichberechtigung jedes Bürgers, jeder Religion, die Freiheit der Industrie usw. Wir finden überall wenigstens die Entwicklung dazu."

[23] "Wie können einer besseren Zeit die Früchte der alten zu erhalten suchen."

[24] Leopold von Ranke, *Aus Werk und Nachlass*, ed. W. P. Fuchs and I. Schieder, vol. 4, *Vorlesungseinleitungen* (Munich, 1975), 467 (from the introduction to a lecture course on the history of the nineteenth century, given in 1869).

He saw in the slow emergence of a common society of nations the promise of the formation of a functioning international system, and this belief in a meaningful course of historical events stood behind his great scholarly undertaking, the writing of a universal history. But if the work of the one became the embodiment of cultural history, the work of the other that of political history, it should not be forgotten that Ranke and Burckhardt had a common bond: the determining factor in their historical efforts was the wish to preserve the heritage of Europe.

Since Ranke's and Burckhardt's times, history has extended its horizons. Europe is no longer the sole or the primary center of attention; every part of the globe has become the concern of historians. With European developments placed in a broader context, Europe may have lost its uniqueness, but it has assumed more individual features. History has also become concerned with the importance of activities and situations that previously had been regarded as being of little significance. In the past, historians focused on leading personalities in politics and war, in intellectual and artistic life, and on the movements in which they had been formed or which they represented. Now the entire population—the way in which they lived, the manner in which they thought—has become an object of study. History has moved closer to economics and sociology, to the social sciences.

Even though the scope of history has been widened since Ranke's and Burckhardt's times, their writings convey a crucial message. They have shown that behind the study of the past there rests an issue with which history is and must be concerned, that of the values underlying and determining human action. History is uniquely important in forcing the reader to look beyond the course of events and to see the decisive role that the choice of values plays in human development.

INDEX